Cambridge Elements

Elements in Historical Theory and Practice
edited by
Daniel Woolf
Queen's University, Ontario

RACE, GENETICS, HISTORY

New Practices, New Approaches

Alexandra P. Alberda
The University of Manchester

Njabulo Chipangura
Maynooth University

Lara Choksey
University College London

Jerome de Groot
The University of Manchester

Maya Sharma
Ahmed Iqbal Ullah RACE Centre and Education Trust

Shaftesbury Road, Cambridge CB2 8EA, United Kingdom

One Liberty Plaza, 20th Floor, New York, NY 10006, USA

477 Williamstown Road, Port Melbourne, VIC 3207, Australia

314–321, 3rd Floor, Plot 3, Splendor Forum, Jasola District Centre, New Delhi – 110025, India

103 Penang Road, #05–06/07, Visioncrest Commercial, Singapore 238467

Cambridge University Press is part of Cambridge University Press & Assessment, a department of the University of Cambridge.

We share the University's mission to contribute to society through the pursuit of education, learning and research at the highest international levels of excellence.

www.cambridge.org
Information on this title: www.cambridge.org/9781009635356
DOI: 10.1017/9781009635363

© Alexandra P. Alberda, Njabulo Chipangura, Lara Choksey, Jerome de Groot and Maya Sharma 2025

This publication is in copyright. Subject to statutory exception and to the provisions of relevant collective licensing agreements, no reproduction of any part may take place without the written permission of Cambridge University Press & Assessment.

When citing this work, please include a reference to the DOI 10.1017/9781009635363

First published 2025

A catalogue record for this publication is available from the British Library

ISBN 978-1-009-63535-6 Hardback
ISBN 978-1-009-63537-0 Paperback
ISSN 2634-8616 (online)
ISSN 2634-8608 (print)

Cambridge University Press & Assessment has no responsibility for the persistence or accuracy of URLs for external or third-party internet websites referred to in this publication and does not guarantee that any content on such websites is, or will remain, accurate or appropriate.

For EU product safety concerns, contact us at Calle de José Abascal, 56, 1°, 28003 Madrid, Spain, or email eugpsr@cambridge.org

Race, Genetics, History

New Practices, New Approaches

Elements in Historical Theory and Practice

DOI: 10.1017/9781009635363
First published online: October 2025

Alexandra P. Alberda
The University of Manchester

Njabulo Chipangura
Maynooth University

Lara Choksey
University College London

Jerome de Groot
The University of Manchester

Maya Sharma
Ahmed Iqbal Ullah RACE Centre and Education Trust

Author for correspondence: Jerome De Groot, Jerome.Degroot@manchester.ac.uk

Abstract: This Element, about historical practice and genetics, seeks to understand what is at stake in presenting, preserving, and articulating the past in the present. Historical practice is both conceptual and material, a consonance of approach which is reflected in the innovative and non-traditional format of the Element itself – not simply in its length, but in its constitution. The Element was created collaboratively with contributions from a range of disciplines, backgrounds, and areas of professional expertise. It consists of a series of interventions which are then discussed by the contributors and is foundationally multi-voiced and discursive. The Element attempts to be non-extractive, ethical, inclusive, collaborative, and constantly ongoing and provisional in its representation. The Element strives to contribute to ongoing attempts to rethink, reconfigure, reassess, and entirely change the object of study and the practice of history.

Keywords: race, genetics, history, museum, curation

© Alexandra P. Alberda, Njabulo Chipangura, Lara Choksey, Jerome de Groot and Maya Sharma 2025

ISBNs: 9781009635356 (HB), 9781009635370 (PB), 9781009635363 (OC)
ISSNs: 2634-8616 (online), 2634-8608 (print)

Contents

Introduction: Genetics, Race, and History   1

1 Jerome de Groot: DNA Reconfiguring Knowledge Structures   11

2 Maya Sharma: How the UK Heritage Sector *Could* Take a More Ethical and Anti-racist Approach to Our Collective Histories   23

3 Lara Choksey: Composite Genomic Portraits   38

4 Alexandra Alberda and Njabulo Chipangura: Towards the Rehumanisation of Ancestors from Colonial Contexts at Manchester Museum   50

Endings   64

Bibliography   68

Introduction: Genetics, Race, and History

This Element, about historical practice and genetics, seeks to understand what is at stake in presenting, preserving, and articulating the past in the present. For us, *historical practice* is both conceptual and material, a consonance of approach which is reflected in the innovative and non-traditional format of the Element itself – not simply in its length, but its constitution. The Element was created collaboratively with contributions from a range of disciplines, backgrounds, and areas of professional expertise. Our contributors are from a range of organisations, all based in the United Kingdom (Njabu moved to Ireland after the Element was finished), and the differences between us are something we explore and celebrate here, arguing that in the articulation of this difference might be the beginnings of true collaboration. The Element consists of a series of interventions which are then discussed by the contributors, and it is foundationally multi-voiced and discursive. It is collaborative and unfinished, a conversation suggesting new configurations and associations. The discursive moments between sections expose our discussion to view and show the differences between approaches. We have attempted to be non-extractive, ethical, inclusive, collaborative, and constantly ongoing and provisional in our representation. We strive to contribute to ongoing attempts to rethink, reconfigure, reassess, and entirely change the object of study and the theory and practice of history.[1]

Throughout our work we use genetics as a means for thinking around what is at stake in undertaking work in history and heritage right *now*. This approach allows us to challenge the fundamentals of institutionalised knowledge systems, and to present reconfigured and newly articulated approaches to understanding, presenting, and studying the past. For us, institutionalised knowledge accretes around the concept of genetics and DNA, presenting us with an urgent example of the ways in which power and violence are inherent in historical articulations of all kinds. We present a set of approaches to race and genetics as a means for challenging existing normative assumptions about the study and practice of history. Our approach looks at race, decolonisation, and genetics to critique existing practice and to posit ways of changing the action of approaching, narrating, articulating, and preserving the past. The Element brings together insights from multiple points of view to reconsider and interrogate issues that might seem clear (DNA *is* truth!) but in reality are not. We consider the implications of genetics in historical, archival and heritage contexts to undertake this interrogative work. This interrogation also enables us to introduce and bring together multiple other ideas and issues, from ethics to metaphor, to

---

[1] Behm, Fryar, Hunter et al., 'History on the Line: Decolonizing History', 169–91.

showcase a suite of approaches to race, genetics, and history emphasising multiplicity, incompleteness, and complexity.

Collaboration and Innovation

Decolonisation entails democratising decision-making and acknowledging that museums, archives, universities and other research organisations are not neutral and have played a role in misrepresenting cultures of the 'other' for a long time. Rachel Minott calls this 'the pursuit of false neutrality.'[2] Warwick Anderson asks, 'How should postcolonial and decolonial theories lead us to revaluate evidence, agency, authorship, temporality, and structure in historical practice?'[3] Our approach has been to combine theory and practice in what we hope is a new and innovative way. One of the challenges for humanities, heritage, and historical scholarship and practice in the next decades will be achieving anti-discriminatory multidisciplinary collaboration. Our approach here might be described as anti-racist transdisciplinary collaboration, seeking to break from an academic validation structure for the knowledge included and produced, the methods used, and who is at the centre of the work. Individually our work is based variously in museums, archives, and university departments, so working together has been about discovering collaborative process. We are also all based in the United Kingdom, and the work that we outline here arises from direct engagement with the ongoing violences of imperialism and colonialism, at institutional, cultural, social, and historiographic level. Indeed, this is one of the key issues that we have had to face in our work. Increasingly museums are developing new practices and there are many individual members of staff working to de-centre the museum and whiteness/Eurocentrism. Similarly, but very much more slowly, universities in the United Kingdom are seeking to at least acknowledge, if not address, their intellectual role in European colonialism, their status as key beneficiaries of mass enslavement, and their generally poor record in working equitably with the communities they sit physically next to. This work has yet to bring about radical structural changes and meaningful devolution of power. In contrast, Global Majority–led community heritage organisations like the Education Trust, Sheba Arts, Serendipity Institute for Black Arts and Heritage, or the Black Cultural Archives have a very different starting point, practice, staffing and so on; in many cases they are 'of' communities as opposed to working 'with' communities.

---

[2] Minott, 'The Past Is Now: Confronting Museums' Complicity in Imperial Celebration', 559–74 (559).
[3] Anderson, 'Decolonizing Histories', 369–75 (371).

There is a developing recognition that a multiplicity of approach, method, and understanding is necessary and should be foundational to heritage and historical work.[4] *Doing* this, however, is incredibly difficult given what has just been raised about institutional structures, power relationships, funding models and intellectual traditions. Our own collaboration has been difficult and complex for us all. Sarah Lloyd and Gary Rivett discuss the centrality of 'failure' as a way of thinking about collaborative and co-productive work.[5] This failure is in project design, due to inequality, because of disenfranchisement, and built into the systems of knowledge that at present sustain heritage and historical work.

How can we do this, then, without it being a failure; or, conversely, is failure as good as we might aim for? Or do we need to let go of historic ideas of what success looks like, in academic writing and collaboration, to step outside of the idea of success and/or failure?

Our thinking throughout is intended to outline the ongoing aspect of historical and heritage work, its fluidity and process. This sounds idealistic, but it is important and extremely challenging. To remain generous, to act with care, to recognise and understand, to empathise, to forgive, to release and let go, to rethink ownership and knowledge and authority and privilege, to offer and to seek understanding whilst also recognising the limits of one's own definition of 'understanding' – these are incredibly difficult things to do within historical and heritage spaces, particularly as practitioners are increasingly prey to nationalistic, manipulative and political interference.

Through the process of working together we identified the following keywords as central to our approach: **Mediation/Curation, Provenance, Measurement, Influence, Metaphor, Artefact/Object/Living Cultures**. Each of these words cuts across our various expertise and interventions and allows a connection to be made between our very different approaches and backgrounds. The keywords provide a means for navigating between different approaches and are outlined at the beginning of each section as well as flagged throughout to illustrate points of contact and comparison. These concepts allow us a foundation to rethink what 'history' and 'heritage' are and might be, presenting in a discursive space a set of interventions that seek to highlight existing problems. This approach allows an understanding of the Element as something multiple and flowing, moving between concepts and ideas and seeking to enshrine that mobility as methodology. Throughout we reflect this mobility of approach, alternating theoretically led sections with those that reflect upon applied implications in order to emphasise combining concept with practice.

---

[4] King and Rivett, 'Engaging People in Making History', 218–33.
[5] Lloyd and Rivett, 'Fraught Spaces', 602–36.

The Element begins with a close focus on genetics and history as a potential space for situating new types of knowledge and potential. This opening section by Jerome de Groot considers how genetics has transformed contemporary ways of thinking about race and history, and how this new understanding is problematic but possibly liberating. Jerome's intervention asks whether the advent of new biomolecular-focused humanities is useful in decolonising effort.

Maya Sharma's section develops this by outlining what is at stake in contemporary heritage spaces and introducing research that shows how museums are seemingly resistant to or reluctant to institute the type of change that our approach demands. This opening section, shows us the potential for new commemorative practices and in particular outlines the approach of the Ahmed Iqbal Ullah RACE Centre and Education Trust as a case-study for rethinking priorities and challenging structures through antiracist approaches.

Lara Choksey then develops the Element's key ideas about the relation between history and race by considering metaphors and images in the conception and application of genetic knowledge, looking at how the normative rationality of 'genetics' is reproduced by visualising diseased types of genome. Lara's section takes up our shared interest in challenging projections of social identity onto genetic factors through the eugenicist origins of statistical modelling in genomics.

The closing section by Alexandra Alberda and Njabulo Chipangura presents cutting-edge approaches to working with ancestral remains in existing colonial collections. Through an exploration of the Manchester Museum's developing policies relating to Ancestors Alex and Njabu present a critique of thinking in relation to collections.

Each section is followed by a discussion between us all, highlighting points of connection and difference between our thinking. We bring our thoughts into final focus in the last section, 'Endings', which seeks to articulate the lessons that might be drawn from our work. Each part of this Element articulates material antiracist and decolonial approach to the past, outlining an ethics of care and practice that is achievable and urgent. Throughout we seek to understand genetics, race, remains, memory, and self as bound up in modes and methods of commemoration.

In the remainder of this Introduction, we outline the ways that understanding, commemorating, engaging with and thinking about the past have been challenged and reconfigured in the past decades in order to provide foundations for our thinking throughout, and in particular to throw into relief the collaborative, yet distinctive, contributions we present.

New Ways of Approaching the Past

Sebastian Faulks's 2023 novel *Seventh Son* imagines a contemporary-future in which the DNA of *Homo neanderthalensis* has been mixed with that of *Homo sapiens* to produce a biologically new being:

> It appears from our studies that Number Seven has a different version of consciousness. It's human, it's sophisticated, it's robust. But it's different.[6]

This idea of 'difference' articulates an understanding of genetic identity as foundational to agency and humanness. In genetic terms the new being is a 'hybrid', and Faulks draws on the discovery of new types of archaic humans in caves in Denisova, Siberia. One of these discoveries was reported by *Nature*: 'Mum's a Neanderthal, Dad's a Denisovan: First discovery of an ancient-human hybrid'.[7] This headline outlines the revelatory quality of this research, but also how it opens ideas of inheritance, authenticity, and, in the use of the word 'hybrid', modern conceptions of ethnicity and race.[8]

Faulks's is just one of multiple books, films, and TV series reflecting upon the transformative intervention of genetics into our day to day lives.[9] Increasingly we understand ourselves genetically, and since the Human Genome Project reported in the early 2000s a huge amount of research has been undertaken to conceptualise the human through an understanding of its DNA.[10] Keith Wailoo, Alondra Nelson, and Catherine Lee argued in 2012 that genetics was becoming a common way to understand the past:

> [DNA analysis] makes fundamental, if problematic, claims about the present and the distant past – and as such, the claims, credibility, and applications of the genetic science must be examined closely and in multiple venues.[11]

The genetic information on historical practice, awareness, and imagining needs to be interrogated thoroughly. Wailoo, Nelson, and Lee further argue that 'DNA analysis is re-creating how we know the past and even how we now define the social world'. Our Element seeks to understand this 'recreation' in relation to historical understanding, practice, and imagination. Consideration of different modes of 'reading' the past reconfigures our understanding of what that past is, how it is constructed, and what it might mean. The increased visibility of genetic work and its wider popular and public impact have led to a profound shift in our understanding of the materials and evidence of the past, and greater

---

[6] Faulks, *Seventh Son*, p. 231.
[7] Matthew Warren in *Nature*, 22 August 2018, nature.com/articles/d41586-018-06004-0.
[8] M'charek, *The Human Genome Diversity Project*.
[9] Hanson, *Genetics and the Literary Imagination*.   [10] Reardon, *Race to the Finish*.
[11] 'Introduction', pp. 1–12 (p. 7).

awareness that we need to reconceptualise our methods and approaches in the humanities accordingly. Understanding the way that genetics has shifted our awareness is a challenge but also an opportunity, as new approaches enable us to reconceive and interrogate old and problematic approaches to narrating and knowing history.

As the previous discussion of 'hybrid' shows, any work that considers genetics and history is ineluctably bound up with race.[12] Evelynn Hammonds argues forcefully: 'We are in the middle of a debate about the power and authority of genetic information and the meaning of race.'[13] In 2004 Jenny Reardon critiqued the Human Genome Diversity Project, an offshoot of the Human Genome Project that sought to create an archive of genetic data to demonstrate human diversity. The pushback to this project from Indigenous, Native, and Global Majority communities demonstrated the problems inherent in contemporary scientific thinking about human genetic variation. Reardon's account demonstrates the centrality of power relations to an understanding of genetic definitions and reminds us that science does not happen in a vacuum:

> Far from allowing us to move beyond race, as many have hoped, these studies instead only highlight the centrality of racial categories in the human sciences. Debates over their meaning and proper definition will continue to be pivotal to determinations of what defines human identity at the level of the genome, as well as which human groups are entitled to full rights of voice and representation at the societal level (Reardon, *Race to the Finish*, 8).

Kim TallBear similarly challenges the imposition of genetic templates onto peoples and communities in the pursuit of a particular type of knowledge.[14] TallBear situates discussions of genomic research within wider understanding of biocolonialism and the historical experience of Native and Indigenous peoples. Her work seeks to develop a framework for Indigenous and Native governance and ownership of genetic materials. The biocolonial impulse to prospect and harvest data from biomatter is driven by need to articulate types of identity and understand human diversity. Without new methodologies, epistemologies, and practice, such research simply reiterates existing power structures.

Challenging and Addressing Colonial Violences through Decolonial Practice

At the same time, the very idea of what history is, what it does, and how it works is being reassessed. Ethan Kleinberg, Joan Wallach Scott, and Gary Wilder

---

[12] See Benn Torres and Torres Colón, *Genetic Ancestry*.
[13] Evelynn, 'Straw Men and Their Followers', pp. 403–409 (p. 408).
[14] TallBear, *Native American DNA*.

remind us that 'existing hegemony is maintained by a nominal pledge to diversity which aims to co-opt rather than transform'.[15] It is crucial to develop robust and challenging models of investigation.[16] In 2018 the American Historical Association introduced new policies for *American Historical Review*. This was an attempt to address 'decades of exclusionary practice'.[17] Alex Lichtenstein argued that they needed to take the is such action sufficient? As many scholars have argued, decolonisation of history can only be achieved through radical rethinking about what 'history' is. The ongoing challenges to power structures, institutions, and material practices of history and heritage demand a sustained, multiple, and material response:

> risk of confronting its own potential complicity in the inability of the profession to divest itself fully of its past lack of openness to scholars and scholarship due to race, creed, gender, sexuality, nationality and a host of other assigned characteristics. ('Decolonizing the AHR', xv)
>
> Fundamentally, any process of decolonization requires us first to recognize the epistemic violence inherent in conventional histories – thereby challenging claims of absolute sovereignty, possession, or universality – and to interrogate simple diffusionist narratives.[18]

The Transatlantic Slave Trade forcibly took Africans from their homes to profit from their sale and forced labour. Enslaved Africans were systematically prevented from holding onto their language, their religious and spiritual practices, their music, clothing, and other cultural practices. Slavers did this for practical reasons: mixing Africans from different language groups made it harder for bonds to form or for other forms of resistance. Prohibiting use of African languages undermined resistance. Colonial powers worked in similar ways, acquiring territories through violence and economic power, and imposing their languages and religious practices. Pre-existing epistemologies and cultural practices were often wiped out or at best depicted as primitive, childish and unsophisticated, or unhealthy and unhygienic.

There was a conscious project to strip people of their distinct cultural practices, removing both their individuality (identity) and their community.[19] Ngũgĩ wa Thiong'o shows how the colonial project used first violence to subjugate people, then forced enculturation and prohibition of language and cultural practices to control both enslaved Africans and Indigenous communities:

---

[15] Ethan, Scott and Wilder, 'Theses on Theory and History', 157–65 (159).
[16] Tuck and Yang, 'Decolonization Is Not a Metaphor', 1–40 and Sailiata, 'Decolonization', pp. 301–308.
[17] Lichtenstein, 'Decolonizing the AHR', xiv–xv.
[18] Anderson, 'Decolonizing Histories', 372. [19] Elkins, *Legacy of Violence*.

> The effect of the cultural bomb is to annihilate a people's belief in their names, in their languages, in their environment, in their heritage of struggle, in their unity, in their capacities and ultimately in themselves. It makes them see their past as one wasteland of non-achievement and it makes them want to distance themselves from that wasteland. It makes them want to identify with that which is furthest removed from themselves, for instance, with other peoples' languages rather than their own. It makes them identify with that which is decadent and reactionary, all those forces that would stop their own springs of life. It even plants serious doubts about the moral righteousness of struggle. Possibilities of triumph or victory are seen as remote, ridiculous dreams. The intended results are despair, despondency and a collective death-wish[20]

To understand this trauma, extraction, and violence as ongoing, and as inculcated and articulated in our historical practices and heritage spaces is both the challenge and the means to future practice.

Collecting practices of the nineteenth century were associated with violence and dispossession. Museums, universities, archives, and other research institutions in the colonial world 'originating in the 16th century with the emergence of Atlantic commercial circuits, had and still have a role to play in the colonisation of knowledge and being'.[21] Some of this Element focuses on the conservation and presentation of problematic cultural heritage objects and Ancestors from colonial contexts that are contained in encyclopaedic museums. We regard these museums as cultural institutions still predicated on the authorised heritage discourse (AHD) that gives power and authority to curators as experts with knowledge to determine what is worthy to be conserved and which cultural stories are presented in exhibitions.[22] Such museums (like that in Manchester), with their preoccupation with scientific taxonomies and ethnographic categorisations, have always been seen as major outposts for producing narratives of progress and rationality.[23] The whole idea of the encyclopaedia is defined here as a colonial legacy in itself for its attempt to both own and represent the world. These museums present an assemblage of the world through their collections that are seen as proofs of colonialism's materiality. In essence in this Element we present encyclopaedic museums as colonialism's tangible manifestation, and as complicit recipients of Ancestors from the colonised people dehumanised to legitimise imperial expansion and domination.[24]

Ivan Karp and Corrie Kratz, examining the role of ethnographic museum in presenting cultural heritage objects of the 'other', distinguished two forms of

---

[20] wa Thiong'o, *Decolonising the Mind*, p. 3.
[21] Mignolo, 'Museums in the Colonial Horizon of Modernity', pp. 71–85 (72).
[22] Smith, *Uses of Heritage*.
[23] White, *Museums and Heritage Tourism: Theory, Practice and People*. Basu, 'Towards the Pluriversal Museum: From Epistemic Violence to Ecologies of Knowledge', 1–16.
[24] Oswald, *Working through Collections*.

authority in museums: the ethnographic authority and the cultural authority.[25] They argue that ethnographic authority comes from the need of researching other people's culture through sustained processes of looting and appropriating heritage using salvage ethnography as a pretext wherein museums would act as saviours of the would be extinct.[26] Cultural authority is a fundamental resource that museums use to produce and reproduce themselves through authoritative exhibitions. However, according to Laurajane Smith, getting to know people's experiences about the past is more important than ascribing their heritage to authorised discourses where expert knowledge has complete hegemony. Instead, she argues that this authorised structure of knowledge can be diffused by acknowledging histories from below and the various socio-cultural processes that resulted in the making of the objects.[27]

We reiterate that the binary division between tangible and intangible heritage is artificial because under most circumstances it is literally impossible to separate practices from material culture.[28] Objects are not frozen in some kind of timeless past but rather are reordered are living beings connected to the present and future in continuous ongoing relationship.[29] These objects connect people, places, and events and represent histories of continuity and change. The idea of heritage in museums is usually associated with the visual presentation of objects of the 'other' in authoritative exhibitions.[30] These problems allow us to challenge the fundamentals of institutionalised knowledge systems, and to present reconfigured and newly articulated approaches to understanding, presenting, and studying the past.[31] Heritage is an affective and performative process in which meanings are continuously made and remade. Henceforth, museums as heritage places become theatres of contested memories.[32] For us, institutionalised knowledge accretes around the concept of genetics and DNA, presenting us with an urgent example of the ways in which power and violence are inherent in historical articulations of all kinds.

A decolonial perspective acknowledges that objects are not mundane but rather represent the coming together of a multiplicity of factors.[33] In this regard, decolonisation means challenging and dismantling colonial structures through

---

[25] Karp and Kratz, 'The Interrogative Museum', pp. 279–99.
[26] Basu, 'Material Culture: Ancestries and Trajectories in Material Culture Studies', pp. 370–90.
[27] Smith, 'Heritage, the Power of the Past, and the Politics of Misrecognition', 623–642.
[28] Zhu, *Heritage Tourism: From Problems To Possibilities*.
[29] Golding and Modest, 'Thinking and Working through Differences: Remaking the Ethnographic Museum in the Global Contemporary', pp. 90–106.
[30] Zimmerer, Odenwald and Todzi, 'Displacing the Objects of Others: Towards a Holistic Approach in (Post-) Colonial Provenance Research', pp. 3–31.
[31] Kirshenblatt-Gimblett, *Destination Culture, Tourism, Museums and Heritage*.
[32] Smith, 'Heritage, the Power of the Past, and the Politics of Misrecognition', 623–42.
[33] Chipangura and Chipangura, 'Community Museums and Rethinking the Colonial Frame of National Museums in Zimbabwe', 36–51.

sharing control and authority in storytelling with originating communities whose cultural objects are contained in museums.[34] In this Element we present a decolonised practice, which is collaborative, dialogical, and sympathetic to different perspectives as it provides a framework for discussion and knowledge production through rehumanisation. Rehumanisation is a proactive approach of acknowledging how both Ancestors from the colonised were dehumanised by different colonial collecting practices spanning appropriations, looting, salvage anthropology, missionary led collecting, grave robbing, theft, plundering and stealing. However, one cannot decolonise and rehumanise without delinking the colonial matrix of power, since the practice of collecting and classifying objects and Ancestors was deeply embedded in colonialism itself which created institutions of power as we know them today.[35]

Incorporating knowledge and experiences form the previously marginalised local communities has potential for freeing the colonial museum and other cultural organisations from being seen as exclusive spaces of difference and cultural representations.[36] This cannot be simple, and must be wide-ranging. Françoise Verges warns us that we must not content ourselves with just diversifying what is on display and/or take pride in increasing the 'so called' diversity programmes.[37] Instead, decolonisation is a programme of absolute disorder that recognises that a museum is not a neutral place but a site of constant ideological, political, and economic battles.[38] Bruno Brulon Soares argues for an anticolonial museum that fully recognise the ever presence of the 'other' who are now here to stay and to share their voices by contesting authorised narratives that previously excluded them from their cultural heritage contained in ethnographic museums. Soares also presents a radical revision of how to decolonise museum purposes and practices by positing that the decolonial question in museums must not premised on its instrumental and pacifying common metaphoric usage. He reminds us that we must confront disturbing histories that were fundamental in the West's riches and resources and its current dominant global position. The West still occupies this position of power and control, and denying this has become politically expedient, as Sathnam Sanghera argues:

> decolonisation cannot just be about restitution or giving back cultural heritage objects to communities – rather it should be about inviting these

---

[34] Chipangura and Seabela, 'Community Collaborations and Social Biographies of Museum Collections from Colonial Contexts: Meanings of Zulu Beadwork', 16–30.

[35] Vawda, 'Museums and the Epistemology of Injustice: From Colonialism to Decoloniality', 72–79.

[36] Soares, *The Anti Colonial Museum*, p. 5.   [37] Verges, *A Programme of Absolute Disorder*.

[38] Verges, *A Programme of Absolute Disorder*.

communities to change our ways of thinking to rethink our own understanding of cultural heritage and denounce the violence produced by museums[39]

The manner in which our imperial history inspires a sense of exceptionalism results in dysfunctional politics and disastrous decision-making. Our collective amnesia about the fact that we were, as a nation, wilfully white supremacist and occasionally genocidal, and our failure to understand how this informs modern day racism, are catastrophic.[40]

To challenge and revise, and to decolonise with the long-term transformation of knowledge, methods, and everyday practices in mind means seriously and exhaustively interrogating our cultural, social, and memorial institutions, and our means of writing, articulating, and sharing insight and understanding. This is what we attempt in what follows.

1 DNA Reconfiguring Knowledge Structures

Jerome de Groot

Keywords: Influence, Metaphor, Artefact/Object

Overview

Genetic science seems to offer new epistemologies that must be conceptualised and understood. This is part of a broader attempt to develop critical and philosophical models that take account of the material, the physical, and the biological. These studies look at the interrelationships between human, self, mind, material, object, and the formation of something called 'history'.

How does considering race, history, and genetics allow us to challenge, open up, define, question, debate and possibly practice a type of 'decolonisation'? How does this shift in information and data about the past enable us to challenge understanding of knowledge and knowledge production, to shift the centres of historical evidence and understanding?

Introduction

In 2022 Svante Pääbo was awarded the Nobel Prize for Medicine. A Press Release from the Nobel Foundation outlined Pääbo's Ancient DNA (aDNA) work and its contribution to establishing 'an entirely new scientific discipline, paleogenomics'.[41] The recognition of Pääbo's work is the culmination of two decades of exponential growth in aDNA work. This research has transformed how we understand human prehistory by analysing the genetic remains found in

---

[39] Soares, *The Anti Colonial Museum*, p. 6. [40] Sanghera, *Empireland*, p. 208.
[41] Press release at nobelprize.org/uploads/2022/10/press-medicine2022.pdf.

archaeological sites. It changes historical understanding but is reliant on genetic analysis of contemporary populations. Articles on aDNA see it as a 'transformative technology ... providing information that is *comparable in power* to archaeology and linguistics'.[42] David Reich argues 'There is now another way to read our pasts' claiming that DNA has been 'transformed into a historical source, a text to pore over'.[43] The impact of this work, it is claimed, is huge; its influence on the way we think about the past and about humanness has been great over the past decade.[44]

The Nobel Press Release suggests that work inspired by Pääbo's research continues to look at the differences between types of *Homo*, 'analyzing the functional implications of these differences with the ultimate goal of explaining what makes us uniquely human' (Nobel Press Release). The Nobel Prize press release was illustrated with an image of this particularity, as *Homo sapiens* was shown shifting away from the evolutionary dead ends of other hominims to generate culture, exploration and trade.[45] As here, aDNA work is often conceptualised as connected to the contemporary and illustrated as part of a progress towards 'now'. Reporting about Pääbo's prize win shows some of the other tropes associated with this type of research. CNN called him an 'Ancient DNA hunter', Reuters led with his 'decoding ancient DNA' whilst *Le Monde* used 'deciphering the Neanderthal genome'. Work in this area is regularly conceptualised in such terms which demonstrates our cultural obsession (and anxiety) about genetic science and history.

Ancient DNA work evades the standard 'sites' of historical knowledge. The material is found in labs, in samples taken from archaeological digs, in bones. It is both part of the contemporary body and yet somehow also millennia old. It can be deeply problematic as a source of historical evidence and information, from dubious practices in collection and analysis, to dehumanising Ancestor 'remains', to ethical queries about working with contemporary Indigenous populations.

At a different end of the historical spectrum cheap Direct-to-Consumer Genetic testing has led to an explosion in genetically defined ancestry and identity. Such data is used to give family history users a sense of their ethnic background defined through their genetic profile. AncestryDNA, the biggest player in this area, advertises in ways that emphasis technological modernity, suggesting that scientific insight can change kinship and challenge normative stories. This revisionist

---

[42] Haak, Lazaridis, Patterson et al. et al., 'Massive Migration from the Steppe', 207–11 (207, my emphasis).
[43] Reich, *A Brief History of Everyone Who Ever Lived*, p. 4.
[44] de Groot, *Double Helix History*.
[45] Press release, 3 October 2022, www.nobelprize.org/uploads/2022/10/press-medicine2022.pdf.

tendency can be seen Ancestry advertising in which technological innovation (represented as data, phones, tablets) provides potential for discovering new kinship groups, cultural heritage, geographical locatedness, and revised understanding of the contemporary world. Advertising shows the complexity of this service, enabling customers to 'discover, preserver and represent' through genetic analysis. The revelatory aspect of this biotechnological intervention is crucial. The new information created seeks to change the way that people think about themselves in the now, and how they relate to their pasts.[46]

DNA data is changing understanding of both ancient and contemporary ends of human existence. Increasingly genetic information and analysis is introducing new paradigms and ways of approaching and understanding the past. Questions of inheritance, belonging, race, ethnicity, and identity are being brought into this discussion, and shared in multiple and complex ways. This raises a number of key issues for historians of all kinds. What are the implications of such expanded genetic datasets for the practice of history? How can genetic data change experience of the past, and our way of conceiving what that past is? How does genetic knowledge challenge normative versions of what historical information might be, or how it might be presented?

Genetic historical approaches can challenge the centrality of race by undermining assumptions, neutralising data and suggesting the modern construction of 'race' is socially and culturally imposed rather than 'innate'. Such techniques decentralise the contemporary, opening up our historical vista substantially. They can also remove the human completely from the story, concentrating instead on pathogens or animals. Genetic complexity, in terms of 'ethnicity', is increasingly understood but this historical diversity is aligned with an ongoing essentialism in terms of the definition of 'race' as will be seen in the following sections. It is now widely understood within and outside genomics that 'ethnicity' is not simply (or at all) a matter of genetics.[47] Despite this, historical markers of race continue to hold power and reproduce old essentialisms.

As we argue throughout this Element, such simplistic and essentialist ideas of race and ethnicity associated with genetic identity often lead to misunderstanding. As Jenny Reardon and Kim TallBear argue:

> In short, while biological anthropologists and geneticists commonly state desires to build an antiracist future, often they do so on conceptual and material terrains that leave intact old links between whiteness and property.[48]

---

[46] Leroux, *Distorted Descent*.
[47] For a discussion of the interaction between culture, ethnicity, and race, see Wade, 'Race, Multiculturalism, and Genomics in Latin America', pp. 211–39.
[48] Reardon and TallBear, '"Your DNA Is Our History": Genomics, Anthropology, and the Construction of Whiteness', S233–S245 (S234).

The commodification of genetics through the intervention of Ancestry and other testing companies highlights this concern with ownership, property, and wholeness.

Yet this huge shift in information and data about the past also enables us to challenge understanding of knowledge and knowledge production, to shift the centres of historical evidence and understanding. Sarah Abel argues that DNA 'is increasingly being used as a tool for piecing together individual and collective histories'.[49] Considering race, history, and genetics allows us to challenge, open up, define, question, debate and possibly practice a type of decolonisation wherein normative knowledge is undermined and a bodily understanding of the past is substituted.

Writing about new genetic approaches to pathogens in history, Monica H. Green argues:

> The new microbiology matters not simply because it solves the question 'What was the disease?', in solving that question (as I believe it does) it opens up entirely new questions, ones we did not previously know we needed to ask.[50]

This sense of 'entirely new questions' being enabled and prompted by aDNA interventions is crucial. Genetic approaches seem to present new answers to old questions, and entirely new questions. In the past decade multiple fields have been created: biocodicology, paleoprotenomics, paleoarchaeology, paleogenetics. These areas have been well funded and supported. Major journals like *Nature* and *Science* have expanded and driven these fields, giving them exposure, and heightening public awareness. What does this huge expansion mean for the practice of history?

The discipline which has had most engagement with genetic approaches is Archaeology.[51] David Reich argues that 'I think what the DNA is doing is it is forcing the hand of this discussion in archaeology'.[52] The approaches have led to a wide discussion about the impact of such work on the field, and of the processes of interdisciplinarity.[53] As one critique has put it, 'the frequent lack of genuine collaboration between fields' is problematic.[54] Thomas Booth suggests a new approach: 'rather than treating these approaches as antagonistic, the discussion can move on to the possible causes of the disparities in cultural and genetic legacies of particular populations'.[55] Others argue that genetics has

---

[49] Abel, *Permanent Markers*, p. 188. [50] Green, 'Taking "Pandemic" Seriously', 27–61 (29).
[51] See Vander Linden, 'Population History in Third-Millennium-BC Europe', 714–28 (714).
[52] Quoted in Zhang, 'Ancient DNA Is Rewriting Human (and Neanderthal) History'.
[53] Furholt, 'Massive Migrations?' 159–91.
[54] Johanssen, Larson, Metzler and Vander Linden, 'A Composite Window into Human History', 1118–20 (1119).
[55] Booth, 'A Stranger in a Strange Land', 586–601 (590).

'lifted an interpretative burden from archaeology'.[56] In 2019 the *New York Times Magazine* outlined concerns with the aDNA expansion:

> in practice, the paleogenomicists have totally altered the environment in which prehistory is being studied by everyone. The landscape is dominated by four well-funded, well-connected labs, three of which ... collaborate closely with one another, to the point that some critics accuse them of collusion. The power of these top labs extends to samples, data and even technology: Proprietary chemical reagents let them isolate and enrich ancient samples much more accurately and cost-effectively than other labs can.[57]

The future of this type of research seems to be intensely collaborative, and models of working will have to be developed to enable such approaches. However, as outlined earlier, the logistics of research raises substantial questions: What does real collaboration look like, and how can it be articulated? How does actual interdisciplinarity work on an institutional level? Where is the power in the relationship? Anthropology and Archaeology have moved as disciplines to think through the ethics and configurations of genetic-based scholarship.[58] For history, heritage, and public history approaches there are substantial challenges to working with genetic evidence and data. It might be argued that archaeology is a science-facing discipline, comfortable with lab-based approaches.[59] History, though, is not. The refiguring of the archive which is happening through the intervention of aDNA and other genetic historical work demands a new set of tools for analysing, understanding, and approaching the past.

DNA Results Revealed on YouTube

On August 12, 2017, the feminist channel As/Is posted a video entitled 'We Took A DNA Test' in which presenters Freddie, Chantel, Devin, Kristin, and Jen spat in a tube live and talked to a representative of a genetic ancestry company about the results generated.[60] The film has nearly 9 million views and over 12,500 comments on YouTube. The emphasis is on matriarchal community:

– and we can actually take a look in your ancestry timeline where that came about, starting with your mother and going back to her mother and her mother and her mother.

---

[56] Kristiansen, Allentoft, Frei, et al., 'Re-theorising Mobility and the Formation of Culture', 334–47 (335).
[57] Lewis-Kraus, 'Is Ancient DNA Research Revealing New Truths?'
[58] See Bolnick, Raff, Springs et al., 'Native American Genomics and Population Histories', 319–40.
[59] See Larsen, *Bioarchaeology*.
[60] 'We Took A DNA Test' at youtube.com/watch?v=39qDQ0chwOk&ab_channel=As%2FIs.

- It's the women. – The women.
- The mothers.
- So your maternal haplogroup is T1A.
- That's good, that must be the best, it's T1A.
- All of the members of T1A can trace their maternal lines back to a woman who lived in the Middle East about 14,000 years ago.
- I got a little emotional when you said we could track our history back to one woman, it's like one great-great-great-great-great-great times infinity grandma. This is really really cool and I wish I could shout out to my old grandma, T1A

('We Took A DNA Test').

Claiming a maternal lineage introduces contemporary political agency, an emphasis on matriarchal identity, and historical inheritance over millennia.

The influencers making these films have tie-ins with genetic test providers and contribute to the wider awareness of historical genetics aligned with 'biotechnological hype'.[61] There are hundreds of individual films uploaded onto YouTube and TikTok of users discussing their own DNA test results and how they make them feel.[62] The complex performative selfhood of social media is inflected by direct to camera unboxing of results and live interpretation of that data. In the As/Is film Freddie claims: 'that is me on that computer screen', articulating an understanding of genetic data as somehow originary. They directly suggest this by pointing at the image, participating in the ongoing conflation of phenotypic diversity as genetic diversity.

What the hundreds of films shared on these topics show is the huge distribution of genetic tests for ethnicity, and their increasing role in the popular imagination as definitional tools (also be seen by their increasing prevalence in popular television, particularly crime drama). Kits that were made initially to support genealogical investigation are routinely used as a means for understanding ethnic history.[63] A key aspect of the online films is the potential for revelation through this means of understanding the self, in particular around race and the potential to discover a 'different' racial identity that has been somehow hidden.[64] There are multiple films of people claiming particular ethnic heritage as a consequence of DNA tests. This social media phenomenon illustrates the complex ways that genetic testing has contributed to

---

[61] Marcon, Rachul and Caulfield, 'The Consumer Representation of DNA Ancestry Testing on YouTube', 133–54 (133).
[62] Basch, Fera and Quinones, 'A Content Analysis of Direct-to-Consumer DNA Testing on TikTok', 489–92.
[63] See de Groot, 'The Genealogy Boom', pp. 21–34.
[64] Geography Now, 'My DNA Heritage Test Results (I Was Shocked)'.

contemporary understanding of historicised race. Not only do the results seem to change the user in the contemporary moment, but they also assign race to historical actors but within a sanitised version of history without power and violence.

The genetic heritage unboxing YouTube phenomenon described here is just one of the most visible consequences of the massive expansion of Direct-to-Consumer Genetic Testing (DTCGT) since 2012. This enables an understanding of genetic history as being something within the user: 'increasing numbers of the public partake in the markets as well as virtual worlds of genetic ancestry and build real-word connections on the 'history in their genes'.[65] Initially large-scale commercial DNA testing was developed by two groupings of companies, one for health profiles (largely 23andMe) and one for family history work (Ancestry.com, FamilyTreeDNA). These tests were designed to connect genealogical users, a means for breaking 'brick walls' in research. They present an alternative means for investigating the past than archival-based work. Genetic ancestry tests give the user information relating to ethnic background, geographical, and possible familial connections to other users. Tests are heavily marketed on aspirational grounds – the user can reconnect, rediscover, and find their true self. They present genetic investigation as more than an adjunct to text-based historical work. DNA is an instant corrective to mistakes, connecting and revising:

> Your DNA can reveal your ethnic mix and ancestors you never knew you had – places and people deep in your past where records can't always take you. Try AncestryDNA, and get a new view into what makes you uniquely you.[66]

AncestryDNA, the biggest provider of such services, has sites across the world and presents information as truly global in scope. These tests are huge business, and the AncestryDNA database is the largest commercial genetic database in the world with over twenty-two million users. The boom in genealogical DNA has led to multiplication of services. There are now widely available tests for multiple users, including for pets and for 'ancient' genetic identity (whether the user is a Viking, Celt, or related to a Queen or King).

The proliferation of these tests popularises genetic historical investigation, making it a new, fun, easy way of thinking about the past, but also something that has the potential to transform identity in the present. This work challenges the centrality of 'historical' approaches, suggesting instead a way of cutting directly to the most important information. It associates genetic profile with

---

[65] Sommer, *History Within*, p. 20. [66] At ancestry.co.uk/.

ethnic identity, and this has become increasingly strong in popular understanding of genetics and history. The tests centre the contemporary participant as the focus of historical investigation, connecting them to the past but changing them in the present. Testing for ethnic and family history is now part of the popular imagination, as TV series such as *Long-Lost Family* (2011–), *DNA Family Secrets* (2021–) and *Finding Your Roots* (2012–) demonstrate.

One of the earliest proponents of DNA testing was the African American historian Henry Louis Gates, Jr. On TV in *African American Lives* and *Finding Your Roots* Gates, Jr. popularised the revisionist potential of genetic testing:

> For generations we have been unable to learn about our African heritage or our family trees. But what if we could trace our roots? What stories would we discover, what ancestors would we meet? What if we could even travel through time, cross the Atlantic Ocean and find where our ancestors were from? Now, thanks to miraculous breakthroughs in genealogy and genetics, we can begin to do just that.[67]

Genetic information can provide connections that were intentionally severed, finding people that were erased, and challenging the centrality of whiteness in the historical account. Such work connects across history and geography, bringing the past closer but also enabling an identification in the present which might be transformative.

By imposing contemporary understanding of ethnicity onto genetic data these tests have led to an understanding of race as something historically understood and comparable to current understanding. One consequence is the opening up of genetics in articulations of ethnic identity. This has led to many people claiming identities, particularly alleging Indigenous, African American, and Native heritage.[68] Alondra Nelson has shown how genetic testing is being used in reconciliation and restitution projects to challenge what she terms 'institutional morality'.[69]

More problematically the use of DTCGT has enabled ongoing ahistorical discussions of racial purity amongst White nationalists.[70] Adam Rutherford argues:

> Reluctance by scientists to express views concerning the politics that might emerge from human genetics is a position perhaps worth reconsidering, as people who misuse science for ideological ends have no such compunction and embrace modern technology to spread their messages far and wide.[71]

---

[67] *African American Lives*, episode 1. [68] Watt and Kowal, 'What's at Stake?' 142–64.
[69] Nelson, 'The Social Life of DNA', 522–37.
[70] Panofsky and Donova, 'Genetic Ancestry Testing among White Nationalists', 653–81.
[71] Rutherford, 'Introduction', paragraph 6.

Rutherford's point reminds us that science is never politically neutral, and that the attempts on the part of genetic science to distance itself from real-world issues has opened up a vacuum in which racist terminology and usage can flourish.

Ancient DNA and Revisionism

Additionally, genetically led history can change the archive of the ancient past. This leads to a revisionism enabling a new way of thinking about what history is and how it is undertaken. In 2017 a Swedish research group published genetic analysis of a body that had been buried in grave Bj 581 in Birka. This famous warrior grave site had been worked over decades. After years of research on the site, osteological data had been used to suggest that the remains were female; genetics was employed to demonstrate that this was incontrovertibly the case:

> The Birka warrior was sequenced to mean 0.09× nuclear and 326.5× mitochondrial genome coverage. The mt-haplogroup was assigned to T2b (Vianello et al., 2013). The total of 11312749 reads mapped to the human genome. When corrected for clonality, the number of reads mapping to X and Y chromosomes were 248,170 and 247, respectively, resulting in the proportion of the alignments (R_Y) equal to 0.001 (SE = 0.0001). The cut-off value for identification of females is $R_Y \leq 0.016$, showing that Bj 581 was a female (Skoglund et al., 2013) (Fig. 3). Hence the individual in grave Bj 581 is the first confirmed female high-ranking Viking warrior.[72]

The process is clear, moving from demonstration of human relatedness to chromosomal sex.[73] The final identification is not just assumed but reliant on other evidence presented by Skoglund et al.

This article was reported across the world. This public and global response is crucial when thinking about the impact of ancient DNA analysis on the way that the past is conceptualised and imagined. It shows the revisionist impulse of reporting in this area when the research touches upon issues relating to modern concepts like gender and race. Two years later the team reflected, 'The buried person has always carried two X chromosomes, even if this was unknown before our recent work; the occupant of Bj.581 will never be biologically male again'.[74] This revisionism suggests Ancient DNA data can change and transform our understanding of human history, subverting received narratives and assumed normative structures. This study shows how the combination of ancient genomics

---

[72] Hedenstierna-Jonson, Kjellström, Zachrisson, et al., 'A Female Viking Warrior Confirmed by Genomics', 853–60 (857).
[73] See also the discussion of gender norms in Frieman, Teather and Morgan, 'Bodies in Motion: Narratives and Counter Narratives of Gendered Mobility in European Later Prehistory', 148–69.
[74] Price, Hedenstierna-Jonson, Zachrisson et al., 'Viking Warrior Women?', 181–98 (191).

and isotope analyses can rewrite of our understanding of social organisation concerning gender, mobility, and occupation patterns in past societies.

On the one hand, this case suggests that genetically based approaches to historical artefacts can challenge long-held assumptions about the past. On the other, it shows how genetics-based history might seem to tend towards a kind of essentialism. This is interesting, given that it initially seems to be introducing a fluidity that reconfigures the past as more complex and challenging to the normative. The focus here is the archive – what it is, how it can be addressed, how it can be challenged, read, constructed, controlled; who has it, who keeps it, who defines it.

The debates over race, archive, and authority can be seen in *Historien om Sverige*. SVT, the Swedish national broadcaster, began its sweeping *Historien om Sverige* [History of Sweden] in winter 2023. The opening featured a group of prehistoric reindeer-hunters. Their leader and the group are played by actors with dark skin, blue eyes, and dark hair. The series suggests that this group is part of what became contemporary Nordic people. The show has led to a wide discussion about the origins of Swedishness and about skin colour and heritage. The programme is led by ancient DNA and archaeological work looking at pigmentation alleles which suggests darker skin in populations from this period and which is also leading to changes in museum practice.[75] SVT had made *De första svenskarna* [The First Swedes] a few years earlier (2019) outlining similar science.

On the one hand this is an intervention into historical understanding of prehistory that is led by genetic evidence, suggesting a non-racialised blackness in prehistory and challenging discourses of whiteness and Eurocentric purity. On the other the show uses re-enactment to perform its historicity and casts actors of African and Asian heritage. They are inescapably contemporaneously racialised and understood even whilst performing and standing in for historically situated people. The show is anti-racist but sustains race-based discussion. This is an example where the presentation of history has been changed by genetic knowledge, but, further, it is a place where historical 'race' enables a discussion and recognition of the embedded historicity of race rather than its inevitability.

Conclusion

New genetic techniques are tools that allow a different configuration of knowledge to be presented and understood. They undermine and change historical knowing and received ideas about the past. This biomolecurisation of the humanities opens a new potentiality for knowledge systems and the institutional

---

[75] Brace, Diekmann, Booth et al., 'Ancient Genomes Indicate Population Replacement in Early Neolithic Britain', 765–71.

power structures that control our historical imaginations. New techniques can produce new archives of information, sources of knowledge that subvert or challenge or obviate older ways of knowing. This might suggest that genetically led 'history' might be something new, a means for challenging and shifting and rethinking, a way of reconfiguring the body in history and of reorienting understanding outside of traditional historiography:

> The analysis of ancient human genomes has emerged as a powerful approach for investigating the relationships of people who lived in the past to each other and to people living today. A consistent theme is that people in any given location across time are usually there as the result of a long history of mobility and interaction. Over the past decade, ancient DNA has provided new evidence – adding to that from other disciplines – refuting myths of the 'purity' of any population and falsifying racist and nationalistic narratives[76]

Jada Benn Torres argues: 'this type of approach can help to fill gaps in knowledge that were created from the destructive effects of colonization'.[77] Furthermore, this might be ultimately a reconfiguration of the way that all knowledge is produced: 'The Indigenous geneticist is the ultimate creator of ethical biovalue and the goal of postcolonial genetic science' (Kowal p. 591).

However this potentiality is within an institutional and political context of oppression and extraction.[78] Susanne Hakenbeck argues that 'geneticists and archaeologists also need to consider the outward-facing consequences of their genomic studies more critically'.[79] Yulia Egorova suggests that whilst it is 'tempting' to conceive of genetic information as something that 'subaltern communities can use as a tool of empowerment in projects of identity arbitration or reconciliation', regularly such projects become a 'tool of subordination, marginalization or oppression'.[80] As we have seen throughout this Element, it is crucial to be vigilant, activist and engaged, as too often archiving, historical and heritage structures simply replace, support, configure, or participate in enforcing unequal power relationships.

Discussion

Maya: There are so many connections here to my thinking about how enslaved Africans were systematically stripped of their heritage, culture, language, roots, and beginning to think how genetic testing might challenge

---

[76] Alpaslan-Roodenberg, Antony, Babiker et al., 'Ethics of DNA Research on Human Remains', 41–46 (41).
[77] Benn Torres, 'Genetic Anthropology and Archaeology', 1–5 (4).
[78] See Fox, 'The Illusion of Inclusion', 411–13 and Tsosie, Fox and Yracheta, 'Genomics Data'.
[79] Hakenbeck, 'Genetics, Archaeology and the Far Right', 517–27 (522).
[80] Egorova, 'DNA, Reconciliation and Social Empowerment', 546–51.

that. It's interesting to reflect on the difference between Black people (who were systematically stripped of their heritage, culture, language, roots through the slave trade) doing DNA tests in order to understand more of their heritage, with the 'Wait, am I Black / Native American?!' group.

Jerome: There is an ongoing movement using DNA tests to demand reparations from those institutions that profited from slavery – for instance, work in the USA by the activist Deadria Farmer-Paellmann. This seems to me an activist way to use genetics in history – like Henry Louis Gates Jr.'s revisionist-geneticist account in *Search of Our Roots*: 'For the first time since the seventeenth century, we are able, symbolically at least, to reverse the Middle Passage'.[81] In terms of the different groups doing tests there is a clear difference in intention and interpretation, and we are in danger of the 'leisure' version of ethnicity-by-DNA becoming so prevalent that it obscures the important work undertaken in various communities.

Lara: I wonder how your writing connects to how Alex and Njabu later talk about ancestral DNA? How do those words 'ancestral' and 'ancient' relate to each other? They seem to be doing really different things. In Maya's thinking about 'cultural DNA' the ancestral seems much closer to community memory and history, whereas ancient DNA is more about species difference and evolutionary 'progress' from one form of man to another.

Jerome: I agree, although everything genetics-related gets overlain on itself I think, so the 'gene' means in multiple ways.[82] The metaphor of DNA and its various cultural meanings are constantly interweaving. In early ancient DNA work the relationship between 'ancestral' and 'ancient' was not well navigated, and increasingly Indigenous and Native communities are seeking to participate and control their data and work on ancestral remains (see the work of the Native Biodata [Consortium]).

Lara: The idea that there isn't a settled sense of historical origin is so suggestive. Presumably at some points some of those sites become more or less trustworthy, as in, is a dig as more plausible possible place of origin as opposed to a lab as place of analysis?

Jerome: For me, this is crucial to the way that the humanities is going to develop in the next decades. Shital Pravinchandra argues that 'Simply put, research in the life sciences is challenging humanities scholars to recalibrate our now customary suspicion of essentialist and deterministic explanations of human society'.[83] Navigating the relationship between the material and its data is changing rapidly.

---

[81] Gates, Jr., *In Search of Our Roots*, p. 10. [82] Rheinberger and Müller-Wille, *The Gene*.
[83] Pravinchandra, 'One Species, Same Difference?' 27–48 (28).

Maya: I'm interested not only in the records and objects collected by museums and archives but especially in the invisible (outside the institute) information: How was this acquired? What was recorded about it? What was not recorded? How is it stored? Does it make its way in exhibitions and public facing work? If so, how is it used? This data often reveals the institution's approach to Global Majority histories, and what it values or doesn't value.

Jerome: So much of public history writing focuses on this wider sense of the development of public information and memory, yet there is a dearth of theory in the field about race and colony. What you seem to be talking about here is about attitude, as well, the ways in which public history and commemoration is so often a practice of extraction (where that extraction is unseen, or unrecorded).

Maya: You've written about the complexities of using genetic testing to somehow fix or pin down ethnic identity, and that this is clearly flawed or simplistic. This makes me reflect on my piece – I use the idea of DNA as a metaphor to critically examine how the heritage sector is documenting our collective cultural DNA via its collections and work with our diverse heritage and histories. Perhaps the use of this metaphor could also be criticised as simplistic?

Jerome: The interaction between the simplistic and the complex in historical imagination and understanding is so crucial. As I argue, genetics *should* bring in ideas of complexity, and contribute a clear understanding of the mass of data abounding. However, it may not do so. What is crucial for us is the investigation of it. As Donna Harraway argued: 'Not only is no language, including mathematics, ever free of troping; not only is facticity always saturated with metaphoricity; but also, any sustained account of the world is dense with storytelling' (Harraway, *Modest Witness*, 64). Without challenging or interrogating these stories, or exposing their origins, they will tend to the normative, the powerful, and the simplistic.

2 How the UK Heritage Sector *Could* Take a More Ethical and Anti-racist Approach to Our Collective Histories

Maya Sharma

Keywords: Mediation/Curation, Provenance, Artefact/Object/Living Cultures

Overview

Museums and archives in the UK make much of their role in recording and telling the nation's collective history. Significant public funding is directed to them for this purpose, with clear expectations that they will work positively with global histories and Global Majority communities.

In this section, I describe how the heritage sector is failing to document or explore our cultural DNA – the histories, memories, experiences, and cultural practices that knit us together as communities. I draw on research carried out by the Ahmed Iqbal Ullah Education Trust (Education Trust) which shows that prevalent practices and attitudes result in museums and archives maintaining a neocolonial position of power. The perpetuation of such structures means that memory is controlled by predominantly White institutions and fails to include Global Majority histories.

I contrast this with examples of work from the Education Trust, where an anti-racist, anti-discriminatory practice centres Global Majority people and communities and shares or hands over power to them. I offer a way of working that – we feel – could result in a more representative, inclusive, and democratic documentation (and exploration) of our collective cultural DNA.

The Ahmed Iqbal Ullah RACE Centre and Education Trust

The Ahmed Iqbal Ullah RACE Centre & Education Trust is a specialist open-access library and archive, focusing on the experiences and histories of Global Majority communities; thinking about race and ethnicity; and anti-racist activism.[84] We are recognised as a centre of excellence in community-led collecting, ethical community engagement, and oral history work. We work ethically and sensitively with Global Majority communities, supporting them to explore, document and share their histories, cultures, and experiences. We also work with the heritage sector, advocating for more ethical and anti-racist collections-based practice, and the building of anti-racist heritage organisations.

The RACE Centre was founded in 1999 in recognition that the experiences and histories of local Global Majority pioneers, activists and communities were not being documented, and that the education system was not equipping young people of all ethnicities to live and thrive in an increasingly multi-ethnic Britain. We exist because of the heritage sector's failure to recognise the UK's ethnic diversity and to ethically and respectfully develop archive and museum

---

[84] By Global Majority, we mean people or communities whose roots are in the Caribbean, Latin America, Africa, Asia, and Oceania, as well as Indigenous people. We recognise that this term isn't perfect but prefer it to the widely used BAME (or BME), as we find it more respectful and inclusive. We only use this term when we wish to talk about a wide range of people and communities, collectively. We use more precise language when we are talking about people from a specific country or community. To understand the complexity of this issue, we recommend the IncArts #BAMEOver statement as a starting point.

collections that reflect this diversity, in all its complexity. The RACE Centre is part of University of Manchester Library Special Collections.

The Ahmed Iqbal Ullah Education Trust was set up as an independent sister organisation, two years later, and leads on in-depth engagement with Global Majority communities and organisations, supporting community-led collecting which results in our unique and rich archive collections. In this section, I will be talking predominantly about the work of the Education Trust.

Contemporary Heritage Sector Practices

The UK population grew increasingly more ethnically diverse into the twenty-first century. The recent 2021 Census in England and Wales established that 18.3 per cent of the population define themselves as Asian, Black, Mixed, and Other (and the variations within that), that is, not White.[85] The group defining themselves as White contains a significant proportion who see themselves as White ethnically but are migrants with their own distinct languages and cultures (e.g. Polish, Ukrainian). How well equipped, then, are our museums and archives to adequately represent and serve this complex and multicultural nation?

To understand this we need to first consider the historic collections the sector works with. Many collections in the UK have overtly colonial roots. However neutral or empiric the collectors considered themselves, the collections – and in particular their catalogues – tell a different story.

The items collected reflect interests or views held by the collector. Collection catalogues were created by people who had little lived experience of the items they were gathering. In most cases they recorded the information that **they** thought was relevant or correct with little or no reference to the people from whom the items were taken. Inevitably, this cataloguing practice crystallises colonial and Eurocentric thinking. Items were often acquired in illegal or dubious ways. The University of Manchester Library Special Collections includes an incredibly rare Guru Granth Sahib. The catalogue includes a note to say an officer of the 52 Bengal Native Infantry had 'wrested (it) from the hands' of a Granthi (Sikh priest) at the Battle of Guzerat.[86] It then made its way through various booksellers and was eventually bought by Enriquetta Rylands in 1901.

Setting aside the colonial nature of many historic collections, we might expect the heritage sector to reflect the wider population change by actively

---

[85] Data at ethnicity-facts-figures.service.gov.uk/uk-population-by-ethnicity/national-and-regional-populations/population-of-england-and-wales/latest/.

[86] Catalogue note at luna.manchester.ac.uk/luna/servlet/detail/Manchester~91~1~441625~274388.

collecting items and records to ensure representation of increasingly multicultural, multi-ethnic experiences and histories. Greater Manchester is one of the UK's most ethnically diverse urban areas: 28.7 per cent of Greater Manchester's population described itself as ethnic minority in the 2021 national census.[87] Local civic institutions make much of this in their rhetoric, strategies describing Manchester as a 'diverse and modern city' and 'a place defined by its diversity, vibrancy and creativity' where its 'commitment to equality and diversity is part of its fabric'.[88] It would be reasonable to expect this diversity to be documented and visible in its local heritage institutions and their collections.

In 2017, the Education Trust set out to see if this was the case. We carried out a piece of research which reviewed museums and archives in Greater Manchester to see how the city region's ethnic diversity was reflected in their collections. We found that only 50 per cent of organisations contacted reported that they had any Global Majority heritage-related material:

> BAME histories are still missing from archives collections across Greater Manchester. While searches in the GM Lives catalogue yield a variety of material, the majority is generic information, unrelated to local populations. Specialist and non-local authority repositories in Greater Manchester hold little, if any material for BAME communities. The following communities appear to be under-represented: Arab, Caribbean, Eastern European e.g. Polish, Baltic States, Irish (mid to late 20th century), Italian, Turkish, Somali, Sri Lankan.[89]

Indeed, many of those surveyed seemed ignorant of relevant materials in their collections:

> Some archives and museums responded to the audit research saying that they held no BAME material. However, our research shows that they do hold material but it is not known about and poorly catalogued. Lack of knowledge about collections and the way they have been catalogued can make BAME heritage appear invisible.[90]

This means that important local histories, which form significant elements of our local and national histories, are absent from our collective records.

Where organisations were delivering Global Majority–focused projects these tended to be for engagement rather than collecting purposes. Institutions aimed to *engage* more diverse audiences but seemed to not see opportunities to tackle

---

[87] Data at greatermanchester-ca.gov.uk/media/8089/census-2021-briefing_ethnicity_final-v5.pdf.
[88] University of Manchester website, http://tinyurl.com/mrzp2rc, Manchester City Council website, http://tinyurl.com/5xhh465f and http://tinyurl.com/3skzbpp5.
[89] At this point we had not shifted to using the term Global Majority. Manchester has sizeable historic Middle Eastern, Eastern European Caribbean, Irish, and Somali communities.
[90] Report at racearchive.org.uk/download/greater-manchester-bame-heritage-audit-summary/.

the gaps or omissions in their collections. In many cases these engagement activities would have resulted in some kind of output (creative work, temporary exhibitions) which seemingly was not seen as worth accessioning into the formal collection.

In *A Tale of Two Cities*, part of the *Guardian* 'Cotton Capital' series focussing on how the history of textiles and cotton in Manchester is told, journalist Lanre Bakare describes the city's 'deliberate amnesia' in relation to its complicated relationship with the Trans-Atlantic Slave Trade.[91] He highlights a striking absence of local Black histories in local museums and offers an alternative vision for the city where Black histories are embraced and centred. The Black histories he refers to, and the life stories presented elsewhere in the 'Cotton Capital' series, draw heavily on archive and library collections held at the RACE Centre. Without these, there would be close to no record of Black activism and the histories of Black communities in local archival memory. Manchester is fortunate to have the RACE Centre – many cities and communities throughout the UK do not have such an institution.

In 2021, we followed our 2017 research with a *national* project looking at racism and anti-racism in the heritage sector. This report, *If Nothing Changes, Nothing Changes*, again examined how the heritage sector approached Global Majority histories, asking organisations how they were documenting Global Majority perspectives and histories. While 61 per cent of surveyed organisations reported looking at their collections to identify and address missing perspectives (or planning to do so), only 23 per cent were actively collecting from Global Majority communities. Over a third of participants saw this as irrelevant.

A picture emerges of a highly selective approach to multicultural and non-White histories, both locally in Manchester and in the UK more widely. While the population grows ever more ethnically diverse the heritage sector seems unwilling to develop its archive and museum collections to document the full range of our multi-cultural multi-ethnic histories.

Selective Programming

It would also be reasonable to expect the sector to deliver events, activities, and exhibitions that present a wide range of Global Majority histories in thoughtful and nuanced ways. Yet in our experience, programming (the public facing activities of the sector, including permanent and temporary exhibitions, events and activities) is frequently deficient. Global histories tend to be presented via temporary projects and exhibitions, often connected to specific commemorative

---

[91] At theguardian.com/news/ng-interactive/2023/mar/31/a-tale-of-two-cities-the-struggle-for-a-black-history-of-manchester.

moments such as Black History Month, South Asian Heritage Month, or Windrush Day. They are often offered as distinct and isolated histories, seldom interwoven through all the stories told by an organisation and excluded from permanent exhibitions.

This was certainly backed up by *If Nothing Changes, Nothing Changes*, indeed our earlier review of Greater Manchester museums and archives found that only 54 per cent of organisations had delivered any kind of Global Majority–focused project work (and note that this was **project**-based).

When Global Majority histories **are** depicted, they are often presented through White eyes for White audiences, reproducing Eurocentric and even colonial views. Community organisations interviewed in our recent research were critical of museum interpretation:

> Whilst interviewees were glad to see their heritage represented, they were critical of curation and interpretation that (re)presented their objects and histories from Eurocentric perspectives. They felt there was often a lack of relevant context, and that the knowledge of White academic 'experts' and curators was valued above people with lived experience of objects and histories (*If Nothing Changes, Nothing Changes*).

The way we tell our collective story has massive blind spots. Exhibitions often draw heavily on colonial collection catalogues so it is hardly surprising that interpretation includes inaccuracies and presents Eurocentric perspectives. Exhibitions skirt around or leave out any reference to traumatic colonial injustices and crimes. Interpretation frequently uses the passive voice and misleading or vague wording is employed which has the effect of playing down or omitting European culpability and brutality. Toxic histories are sterilised, perhaps reducing discomfort for White visitors but leaving Black and Global Majority people wondering where their ancestral experiences actually **are**.

While Global Majority communities have been calling for a more honest and accurate representation of these aspects of our collective histories for decades, the heritage sector is seemingly only now getting to grips with this.[92] What's more, in talking about this work many heritage organisations present themselves as entirely self-correcting and benevolent: there is no mention of the lobbying and persistent calls to do better from Global Majority communities. Their agency and activism are actively excluded.

Ultimately, as there have been very few updates since the flurry of Black Lives Matter statements in 2020 it is hard to see whether there have been significant and widespread changes in the sector. In the words of Ambalavaner Sivanandan, 'we

---

[92] See the Heritage Alliance report, theheritagealliance.org.uk/wp-content/uploads/2021/03/Joint-statement-of-intent-for-the-heritage-sector.pdf.

are here because you were there'.[93] Colonialism and the Transatlantic Slave Trade are integral parts of our collective histories, and if the sector does not honestly engage with and confront these histories, significant parts of national histories are not being told.

Unbalanced and Extractive Relationships with Communities

Our 2021 research *If Nothing Change, Nothing Changes* invited community members to share their experiences of working with the heritage sector. Whilst some reported positive experiences, on the whole a negative picture emerged. It appeared that museums and archives struggled to work in ethical, respectful, and sustained ways with their local communities, and the relationships with community groups often replicated colonial power structures.

Community members repeatedly told us about the **extractive** nature of museums. In many cases, museums expected the community groups they work with to translate and interpret for them, to organise trips and visits to museums, and to use their position of trust and social capital with their communities, with minimal recognition or remuneration. There was little consideration of the emotional impact of working with traumatic colonial histories and collections and no budget or provision for counselling or emotional support.

Community members also reported feeling that museums sought them out for partnership work when it suited the museums or was a priority for them, but that relationships were not sustained once temporary funding came to an end or the museum's priority had changed. This sporadic engagement left them wary of future engagements.

We have also noted that museums seldom treat the outputs of community engagement activities as worth accessioning. On several occasions, local museums have approached us at the end of a project with a collection of items gathered or created during the project, inviting us to take these into our archives. We find ourselves wondering why the museums didn't choose to accession the items themselves, given the unrepresentative nature of their existing collections. This suggests that they don't see the outputs of their community engagement as significant or valuable enough to make space for in their collections, preferring to pass them on to us.

Museum spaces fail to consider and cater for needs. There is often no clearly marked prayer space and no halal/kosher food in the cafe. The food and retail offer is often expensive and does not reflect diverse tastes and interests. This, combined with the lack of thoughtful programming of global histories and cultures, results in museum spaces feeling uncomfortable and

---

[93] Younge, 'Obituary: Ambalavaner Sivanandan'.

unwelcoming. As one community member said: 'I don't really feel like it is my space, when I go there, I feel like I need to leave soon' (*If Nothing Changes, Nothing Changes*).

It is hard to understand how the sector could be failing Global Majority communities when sector funders have increasingly made community engagement and engaging diverse audiences a priority (often a condition) for funding over the last three decades. For example, the National Lottery Heritage Fund made 'a wider range of people will have engaged with heritage' a mandatory outcome for all funded projects in 2018. To this date, we have yet to hear of any projects or museums losing their NLHF funding for failing to serve Global Majority communities well.

Sector Infrastructure

Unfortunately, the heritage sector's challenges relate not only to collections and how they are used, but also to far wider institutional issues that we feel prevent the sector from **accurately** documenting, exploring, and sharing our historical and cultural DNA. *If Nothing Changes, Nothing Changes* identified a number of concerns relating to the infrastructure of the sector.

A major concern, and one that has been repeatedly flagged over decades, is that the workforce is disproportionately White, especially in specialist, middle, and senior roles. Our research found that of the survey respondents that monitored ethnic makeup of their workforce, 58 per cent reported their organisation having 0–5 per cent Global Majority staff and that these staff were most likely to work in lower-level jobs – especially front-of-house or visitor experience roles. Arts Council England collects diversity data from the organisations it funds, and yearly reports show that the museum workforce is consistently the least ethnically diverse of all disciplines in the cultural sector (7 per cent of the museum workforce defined itself as Black, Asian, and Ethnically Diverse in 2020). Just as the sector's collections do not reflect our cultural DNA, the sector workforce does not reflect our multi-ethnic population.

Poor workforce diversity hampers the heritage sector in multiple ways. Community groups who took part in *If Nothing Changes, Nothing Changes* talked about not seeing themselves reflected in the museums they visited which increased their feeling of not belonging. It also means the sector is missing out on the different perspectives and experiences that can enrich its work. If the sector's workforce doesn't reflect the population, this is clearly an inequitable situation and unlikely to be purely a matter of chance.

If Nothing Changes, Nothing Changes also confirmed what we have long observed: that museums and archives rely on external, temporary project-based funding to deliver work focusing on Global Majority communities and histories. Heritage sector interviewees reported that their organisations were extremely reluctant to commit core or unrestricted income to this work and to anti-racist activities. This results in patchy and sporadic activities which make sustained and respectful relationships with community partners extremely difficult. It is hard not to interpret the unwillingness to direct core or unrestricted funding towards activities designed to diversify collections, programming, and audiences as a lack of value for this work and these histories.

Language

These concerns were not, however, that heritage sector respondents felt were the main challenges. When we asked them what held them back in terms of anti-racism and EDI work, they repeatedly described anxieties about language.

Respondents reported feeling unsure about what language to use. For example, some did not know whether BAME was still 'the correct term' and whether they were 'allowed' to use it. They worried that using the 'wrong' language would hamper their attempts to build relationships with Global Majority communities and groups. They were also concerned that the language they used might deter potential volunteers and job applicants. This fear about using the 'wrong' language recurs in the consultancy work we carry out; the starting point for conversations about what the organisations (thinks it) needs is often training in 'the right language and terminology'. Notably, not one community member raised language as a concern in our interviews, choosing instead to highlight extractive approaches and a lack of respect for the skills of community members as bigger issues. We have our own concerns about the language used in the sector. We have seen a move away from using language such as 'racism' and 'anti-racism', 'equality', and 'equity' and towards more diffuse terminology such as 'belonging', 'empathy', and 'compassion'. Whilst we believe that these qualities are important to embody in the sector's work, we feel that if used **in place** of the language of anti-racism, we lose important specificity and urgency. The terms shift us from specific actions that tackle the barriers to Global Majority people and communities. Effectively, we worry that the sector is letting itself off the hook by moving away from the language of action and activism to more comfortable but diffuse language.

Arriving at a More Accurate and Inclusive National DNA

My aim is not purely to describe the inadequacies and failures of the heritage sector in terms of establishing and articulating our multi-cultural collective DNA. Instead, I want to challenge the pervasive idea that it is **difficult** to work towards more accurate and representative collections, and more equitable working practices. By offering examples of the work we do at the RACE Centre & Education Trust and sharing our learning, I hope to show that in fact, there are more anti-racist and inclusive practices that if adopted by heritage sector organisations, could result in a rich and nuanced national DNA.

What Do We Advocate For?

Our ongoing research into EDI and anti-racism in the heritage sector reveals that many heritage sector workers do not really know what anti-racist practices are. Beyond specific actions (for example, diversifying their volunteer group or celebrating Black History Month) they struggled to articulate what a museum or archive that has embraced multi-cultural histories and embedded anti-racism in all aspects of organisational life might actually look like.

We therefore included a description of what we advocate for in *If Nothing Changes, Nothing Changes*. This described how heritage organisations might behave in order to work equitably and ethically with global histories and communities:

- Recognising and decentring Eurocentric and colonial perspectives
- Actively building more representative collections that include diverse voices and perspectives
- Programming and curatorial work that treats Global Majority histories as of interest and relevant to everyone, as well as more targeted and specific work focusing on specific histories and experiences
- An honest and unflinching examination of the origins of our collections, houses, and heritage assets/willingness to address the destructive nature of colonialism and the transatlantic slave trade

We made detailed recommendations on how to how achieve the aforementioned, which would require:

- Genuine buy-in from leadership in heritage organisations, as well as funders
- Building ethnic diversity at all levels of the sector workforce and across different roles
- Ethical and respectful collaboration with community groups
- Creating spaces that are welcoming, inclusive and well-used by Global Majority people

How Might We Get There?

Whilst the practice of the Ahmed Iqbal Ullah Education Trust and RACE Centre is by no means perfect and is always developing, we feel that our community-led collecting model and our engagement practices offer a way forward for the sector. If key practices were adopted by mainstream heritage institutions, the sector would be taking strong steps to a more equitable approach to our collective histories and to building anti-racist organisations.

The *Coming in from the Cold* project (2018–2024) was a significant milestone in our collecting history. Its project's aim was to support Global Majority communities to develop and deliver their own heritage projects, which would result in some kind of archival deposit thereby leading to better representation in local archives. As the project developed so did our practice: we moved more and more towards a democratic and empowering way of working with our community partners. Whilst there are other community or participatory archives that embrace similar ways of working, our practices are overall unusual and seldom seen in more mainstream archives. I will highlight what we consider to be the key components of this community led collecting.

Communities in the Driving Seat

Where museums and archives are working on collecting Global Majority histories this inevitably takes a familiar form: they recognise a gap in their collections, devise a collecting project, and apply for funding from National Lottery Heritage Fund (or similar) to remedy this. If successful they work with Global Majority people or groups to collect items and oral histories to document their histories. The heritage organisation holds the budget, decides what themes or histories it wishes to collect, usually designs the project and its outputs, writes the collection catalogue, and invariably holds onto the ensuring collection. Whilst it is positive that they are actively collecting from communities, this is frequently an extractive approach where communities are placed in a passive role. Furthermore, the ensuing collections are, despite the best intentions, often framed by White perspectives and interests.

Historically, we took a similar approach: we developed collecting projects, secured grant funding, and worked with communities to collect their histories. While we undoubtedly worked in inclusive ways and had strong relationships with community partners, as the project instigator and deliverer we held onto a considerable amount of power: we had control of the finances, the timeline, and activities.

Moving towards a community-led collecting model has meant handing over this power. Rather than applying for funding and delivering projects ourselves we support community groups to secure their own funding. If successful, they hold this funding and deliver the project themselves, with us injecting our archival expertise and knowledge where required. This puts them in the driving seat, in control of their own projects.

We put our archival and other technical skills at the disposal of our community partners and to offer support on other aspects of their projects, if they wish. Although groups often ask for help in developing the *shape* of the project (i.e. how to explore and document their experiences, how they might share these through exhibitions and events), we do not influence how they frame their histories. For us, it is vital that communities define the elements of their histories and experiences they wish to explore and record: they decide what is most valuable to document.

Co-cataloguing with Our Community Partners

Collection catalogues are vital documents, distilling knowledge about collection items and as sources of information when creating exhibitions and using items in engagement and other activities.

While not all cataloguing practice is overtly colonial, much takes neocolonial forms. Typically, the curator or archivist creates the catalogue. This is often a labour of love, a way of channelling and displaying their significant specialist knowledge. They decide on the contents of the catalogue, the language and terminology used, the contextual information, key words and other search tools. Essentially, they decide what is relevant and important and therefore included, and what is not. This means that, despite best intentions, catalogues often capture and re-enact Eurocentric perspectives and value systems and omit lived experience. Global Majority histories are framed and described by White people (often incorrectly or insensitively).

In contrast, the Education Trust's s cataloguing has become a shared process, which we call co-cataloguing. When working with community organisations on their heritage projects we explain the role of the catalogue and how they are created; we offer template paperwork that can be easily adapted for their use. Our archivists then work with community members to create the collection catalogue. This entails a number of meetings to discuss the catalogue. Community members decide what contextual information to record, how to describe the items held in the collection, and identify key words. Our archivist will write this up, creating drafts that community members review and – importantly – sign off.

This can take considerable time and we always work on the community group's timeline. Whilst we are keen to see catalogues complete so the collections can be made publicly available, we are sensitive to the many pressures on their resources and time. In many cases, they will be carrying out this work in an unpaid capacity. We seek to fit around their commitments, sometimes meeting outside work hours if this makes things easier for them.

Overall, this process brings together archival expertise with community knowledge and lived experience, resulting in collections framed by our community partners perspectives and catalogues that capture what they think is important to record. There is a demystifying of the archiving process and a handing over of power and control to community members.

Sharing Spaces

We know that for many of the groups we work with, there is a strong interest in showcasing their projects and sharing their heritage and culture outside their communities. The cost of central locations, however, often prohibits this.

We therefore offer to make space and support them in showcasing their projects, often securing space in Manchester Central Library where we are based (at no charge) for their exhibitions, activities and events. Groups have told us they found this validating: the presence of their histories in a space like Manchester Central Library underlined the significance and value of their historical research and knowledge production.

Communities Speak for Themselves

Being one of a very small number of Global Majority–led and –focused archives, and working in the ways we do, mean that we are frequently invited to speak about our work at events, or through publications. We are pleased to receive this attention and validation and think it is important to share our practice and learning. However, we do not feel it is ethical to take up these opportunities without our community partners as this would centre our organisation and exclude their knowledge, skills, and expertise.

We therefore try to secure invitations for our partners too, asking that they speak/write alongside us with equal recognition. In some cases, we decline invitations, suggesting our community partners in our place. Often this means advocating for their payment: financial recognition of the knowledge they are sharing and of their time. This is not always met with a positive response as in many cases event organisers or publishers are unwilling to find the funds to support community groups' participation.

Unconditional Support

Notably, and in contrast to common sector practice, we make no assumption nor expect that any ensuing collections come to us. Instead, we offer our support and expertise unconditionally to the communities we work with, allowing them to choose the home for the archive collection. One organisation, for example, felt it was important for the archive created by their project to sit in their local authority archive, as there was no other record of Black presence in the area.

For us, the important outcome is that Global Majority communities in Greater Manchester have an archival presence – whether these archives come to us, another archive or is looked after by the community groups we worked with is not important.

Conclusion

In this section, I have used DNA as a metaphor for the UK's heritage and suggested that the heritage sector presents itself as working benignly and diligently to articulate our cultural and ethnic DNA. Through an examination of common practices and by drawing on recent research I have highlighted and illustrated the sector's many blind spots and pointed towards a stubborn unwillingness to work with diverse histories and to honestly confront the sector and the UK's colonial histories.

In contrast, I have shared some of the ethical practice at the Ahmed Iqbal Ullah Education Trust and RACE Centre, where we support Global Majority communities to research and document their histories and experiences. We feel this is the starting point to more representative local and national archives, and importantly, archives that are framed by the subjects themselves. We feel that our collecting practices could be of great value to the wider sector and would result in far more ethical, sensitive, and community-centred ways of working.

Discussion

Jerome: I think that the value of this piece is its palpable anger but with clear data to back it up.

Maya: I *do* feel angry. My organisation has been advocating for more ethical, representative and anti-racist work for so long, alongside countless others and it feels like so little progress is being made. This anger is often used against us, we are told to be less emotional or biased, we can see how unpalatable our anger is within the sector. I find Sara Ahmed's writing powerful on this, in *Complaint!* She examines how the person who raise the problem becomes the problem.⁹⁴ Data is important, not least because it defends us against the charge of being biased or seeing the worst of the sector.

Jerome: I like the idea that the heritage sector has a duty to educate properly and rightly – the input of the UK government after the toppling of the Edward Colston statue in Bristol demonstrated that that independence was possibly illusory.⁹⁵

Maya: When we look at the aims, mission, or objectives of museums in the UK, the majority include reference to education in one form or another. But if we ignore, skirt around or diminish the UK's pivotal role in the Trans-Atlantic slave trade and the impact of colonialism, how can we tell a nuanced and accurate story? What does this mean for the sector that purports to document and tell these stories, to document, explore, and share our cultural DNA?

Lara: It seems as if the idea of DNA as hereditary material (and genes before that) comes attached with so much social meaning. Is 'cultural DNA' a way of unpacking the way popular understandings of genetic inheritance are already so attached to history, memory, experiences and cultural practices of communities?

Maya: I think it's probably impossible to detach the two. The many videos of people receiving their DNA tests results often include them making some connection between their skills, tastes, talents or beliefs and their newly discovered genetic make-up (inheritance).

Jerome: There is a strand of thinking coming through everyone's work about 'new' approaches reordering the archive and challenging the power structures inherent in historical thinking and articulation.

Maya: Absolutely. Though in many cases, colonial collectors placed huge value on the level of detail they gathered and recorded, resulting in catalogues (or other forms of documenting collections) that are widely considered comprehensive. Where these Eurocentric practices are questioned, the sector's response is often to **add in** knowledge or information from modern-day communities. We would argue for a more radical practice that is less about *adding-in* and more about *de-centring* much of what has already been written down in favour of Global Majority perspectives, knowledge, and experiences.

Jerome: Could you outline more about the RACE Centre and Education Trust's understanding of the word 'decolonise'?

Maya: We tend to avoid the term decolonise on the whole. I think it's become really degraded, people use it in vague ways and don't understand that it's a radical act which inherently involves dismantling and rebuilding systems and

---

⁹⁴ Ahmed, *Complaint!*   ⁹⁵ See Fowler, *The Countryside* and Lester, *Deny and Disavow.*

structures. It's a bit like co-curation/creation – now any activity that involves even a glancing reference to a community group is labelled 'co-'.
Decolonising a museum is a transformative process which completely breaks down and re-builds the organisation. Although many museums are making bold moves, as yet much of the work appears to be focused on collections and programming, with little work looking at the power structures built into the organisation or making the workforce truly representative at all levels.

Alex: It is so important to call out and distinguish the lack of representative collecting and how much diversity work is short-term engagement.

Maya: It is; the short-term nature of 'diversity' or 'decolonising' activities is really disappointing. Fundamentally, we won't realise the significant shift we believe is needed for the sector to be operating in truly ethical and representative ways without sustained, root-and-branch work.

Alex: It is also important to note how the idea of 'community' is being used in each of our sections.

Maya: I think we've all approached it slightly differently but all with a strong interest in centring people who have been denied power, voice, and agency.

3 Composite Genomic Portraits

Lara Choksey

Keywords: Mediation/Curation, Measurement, Metaphor, Artefact/Object

Overview

After the first draft sequence of the human genome was published in 2001, molecular biology entered its 'postgenomic' phase, when research on human genetic diseases expanded through the development of new technologies for visualising them. This section is about the longer history of composite imaging techniques dating back to the nineteenth century, and how these 'generic images' created classifications of human types, including those of race and character. While the classifications themselves have fallen out of use, the visualising techniques used to generate them are analogous to those used in genomics to produce images of diseased genomes. This section develops this Element's historical consideration of genetics and scientific racism through the development of what Francis Galton called 'pictorial statistics'.

Introduction

In the late nineteenth century, Francis Galton wrote a series of articles on what he called 'composite portraits'. At first, Galton wanted to find a way to measure what he saw as standard human faculties of perception and recollection (what he called 'sense impressions'), to create averages of an individual's powers of sense impression, and to compare different rates of sense impression among humans. He used photography to create what he called 'generic images' of multiple people by layering photographs over each other. These included criminals and Jewish people, and his aim was to assess and identify the average features of a certain type, in what he called a method of 'pictorial statistics'.[96] While the scientific validity of these methods has long since been discredited, genomics still uses composite images to determine types of disease.

The principle of human types still has some weight and bearing in genomic research, particularly when it comes to ethnicity, despite the consensus that, as Angela Saini puts it, 'the demographic categories we recognise socially do not in fact have very much biological meaning'.[97] In biomedicine, ethnicity categories are crude placeholders that have not been updated significantly since the mid nineteenth century. 'Ethnicity', as it is sometimes used in human genomics, is caught in a circular problem: how to investigate populational differences in predispositions towards particular genetic disorders or susceptibility to environmental influences, while not restating racist ethnic categories invented by scientists like Galton who wanted to explain and justify the racial superiority of Europeans, and to harness the course of evolution to promote the 'best' genetic stock succeeding? That is, what to do with the empirical infrastructure of eugenic ideology, even while the genomic sciences are not explicitly engaged in its practices of biological engineering? What is the line between eradicating types of disease, and types of human?

The draft sequence of the human genome was produced through the combined averages of sequenced genomes from several anonymous donors, all of whom were Caucasian (that is, of European descent. This became the human reference genome, whose universal reliability has been questioned and disproved from almost the earliest days of its publication. In 2019, Sara Ballouz, Alexander Dobin and Jesse Gillis published a paper in *Genome Biology* describing the reference genome as 'idiosyncratic', more like a type specimen than a baseline.[98] It could not represent *Homo sapiens* as a species consistently or reliably, as the architects of the Human Genome Project claimed it could. But while the reference genome is notoriously unreliable when it comes to non-Caucasians it continues to be the global standard in genomics laboratories across the world in periodic updates (we are now on GRCh38). In its own way, the reference genome has

---

[96] Galton, 'Generic Images', 532–44 (538).   [97] Saini, 'Stereotype Threat', 1604–05 (1604).
[98] Ballouz, Dobin and Gillis, 'Is It Time to Change the Reference Genome?'

become a kind of composite image: an average of a small group of people, but not an ideal type corresponding to all of humanity.

Why did the idea of a reference genome yield such power in genomics? To answer this question, we need to look at how the language of average and type became foundational in early statistical analysis.

Comparative Worth and Family Merit

Galton relied on his own identifications of different human types to generate hypotheses about their relative capacities. One of the longer chapters of his early famous work, *Hereditary Genius* (1869), is titled 'The Comparative Worth of Different Races'. There, Galton ranks different types of humans, placing Aboriginal Australians and Black Africans at the bottom, and Athenians at the top. Importantly, Galton still considered the former as human, writing that 'mistakes' that the Africans he encountered during his travels in southern Africa made 'were so childish, stupid, and simpleton-like, as frequently to make me ashamed of my own species'.[99] It matters that Galton considered Africans as fellow humans, if inferior to Europeans, because his project of ranking different humans was directed towards promoting the reproduction of superior types across geographical and historical differences. For instance, he considered men of 'our own race and time' (the mid nineteenth century) to compare unfavourably to the Athenians of the fifth century BC. Where are the Socrates and Phidias of the last 2,000 years, he wonders? 'They are, therefore, two or three grades above our G' (*Hereditary Genius*, p. 342).

Galton's race typology was eccentric. In another chapter, he demonstrates through looking at the family trees of several poets that, as a race of men, they are unlikely to make useful public servants. Creating useful public servants was the organising principle of his new science of eugenics, which he defined as: 'the study of the agencies under social control that may improve or impair the racial qualities of future generations either physically or mentally.'[100] He was fixated on biological heredity, or what he called 'family merit'. Unlike many of his peers, including Darwin, he did not care about what this unit of heredity might be (Darwin called it the 'gemmule', and Wilhelm Johannsen would later call it the gene), but about calculating the rate at which hereditary stock produced 'healthy and long-lived' families.[101] In the 1880s, he thought that

---

[99] Galton, *Hereditary Genius*, p. 339.
[100] Galton, 'Eugenics, Its Definition, Scope and Aims', 1–25 (3).
[101] Galton, *Inquiries into Human Faculty and its Development*, p. 212.

this could be measured by looking at the occupations of a family's male members over three generations, and by measuring their longevity. In *Inquiries into Human Faculty* (1883), he wrote,

> I cannot doubt, if two youths were of equal personal merit, of whom one belonged to a thriving and long-lived family, and the other to a decaying and short-lived family, that there could be any hesitation in saying that the chances were greater of the first-mentioned youth becoming the more valuable public servant of the two. (*Inquiries*, p. 212)

What did Galton mean by 'valuable public servant'? Why might this have been a category of human that he sought to identify and whose lineage he wanted to promote?

Galton did not trust the course of natural law when it came to human evolution. Nature, which as his cousin Darwin had theorised, was subject to chance and could not be trusted to reproduce valuable public servants at random. The greatest race of man, the Athenians, had fallen into history books. In 1907, he gave a public lecture promoting the work that he and his protégé Karl Pearson had been undertaking at University College London. The lecture, titled, 'Probability, the foundation of eugenics', explains and justifies their laboratory's work on eugenics via Pearson and James Weldon's science of biometrics. Galton admitted that his age had prevented him from taking more of an active role in the work at UCL, and began by mourning his old friend Herbert Spencer, after whom the lecture is named: 'Among the many things of which age deprives us, I regret few more than the loss of contemporaries.'[102] The first part of the lecture continues this theme of loss and uncompleted projects, turning to a reading of *Hyperion*, John Keats's unfinished epic fragment about the fall of the Titans. The poem begins with a mournful Naiad weeping at the feet of the old, sleeping Saturn. Galton commends Keats's thoroughness, by which he means the poet's ambition, as he 'makes the very Divinities to be [the work's] product' (*Probability*, p. 7), a scale of enterprise that he may have seen as complementary to his own desire to intervene in the laws of natural inheritance. Saturn is eventually roused and summons his advisors and demands their help, and old Oceanus – who has lost the sea to Poseidon – warns Saturn not to be consumed by wrath, nor 'writhe at defeat, and nurse your agonies'.[103] This fall was inevitable, 'the course of Nature's law', just as those who have succeeding the Titans will fall too: 'by that law, another race may drive / Our conquerors to mourn as we do now' (ll. 230–1). Oceanus makes a Lamarckian case for the perfectibility of natural forms, and that natural law determines that

---

[102] Galton, *Probability, the Foundation of Eugenics*, p. 6.
[103] Keats, 'Hyperion', ll, pp. 173–74.

the future will be better than what has come before. He does not want to quarrel with the march of time, just as 'dull soil' should not quarrel with 'the proud forests it hath fed, / And feedeth still, more comely than itself' (ll. 217–19). It is time to move on, Saturn, Oceanus is saying.

Galton uses Oceanus's warning to Saturn to make a case for men as 'the chief, and perhaps the only executives on earth' (*Probability*, p. 9), and Nature the old form that human invention will transcend. For Galton, eugenics was the man-made machinery that could intervene in and restrain the laws of natural catastrophe, not a consolation for the inevitable. The possession of free will gives men justification to interfere with 'the pitiless course of Nature ... by gentler and kindlier ways' (*Probability*, p. 9). Galton wanted to conquer natural forces; like Oceanus, he believed in the conquest of cultivated beauty over disordered mess, but for Galton this could be engineered by science. Underlying the preoccupations of this lecture – heredity, ageing, battling the forces of natural selection, replacing chaos with order – was the fear that human race might become extinct. Galton wanted to safeguard the species with what he saw as the best of its kind against this by breeding in the best stock.

From Composite Portraits to Generic Image

When Galton gave the Spencer lecture, he was increasingly concerned about the deteriorating quality of British hereditary stock: 'The mentally better stock in the nation is not reproducing itself at the same rate as it did of old; the less able, and the less energetic are more fertile than the better stocks' (*Probability*, pp. 10–11). He was against the idea that this problem of national degeneration could be solved by educating the population; intelligence, for Galton, was hereditary, not a matter of education: 'No scheme of wider or more thorough education will bring up, in the scale of intelligence, hereditary weakness to the level of hereditary strength' (*Probability*, p. 11). The problem could only be solved through selective breeding, and by preventing bad stock from coming into the population. Controlling the means of reproduction was one such method of control.

Pearson's methods of statistical analysis made it possible to determine the rates of good and bad hereditary stock, but well before he met Pearson, Galton had been preoccupied with ways to use composite methods for generating averages. From these averages, it was possible to determine between types of human. His first port of call was to determine rates of sense discrimination: how well certain humans could recall and visualise things they had seen or read (paintings, military reports, cards out of a deck, the arrangement of furniture). In keeping with his arguments in *Hereditary Genius*, Galton thought that certain types of human have higher levels of sense discrimination than others.

In *Inquiries into Human Faculty*, he wanted to show that, 'a delicate power of sense discrimination is an attribute of a high race, and that it has not the drawback of being necessarily associated with nervous irritability' (*Inquiries*, p. 22). Women are worse than men at 'distinguishing the merits of wine', and they are not very good at making tea or coffee either, and in general, 'men have more delicate powers of discrimination than women' (*Inquiries*, p. 22). In his examination of Southern African communities, all were distinguished from civilised White men: 'My own experience, so far as it goes, of Hottentots, Damaras, and some other wild races, went to show that their sense discrimination was not superior to those of white men, even as regards keenness of eyesight' (*Inquiries*, p. 22). Galton wanted to work out how these powers of sense discrimination might be grouped into different types of sense impression. With this catalogue of types of sense impression, it would be possible to measure the level of sense discrimination between different types of humans.

In his criteria of sense impressions listed in a talk to the Philosophical Society of Birmingham in 1879, Galton privileged the visual over the sonic, the olfactory, and the gustatory, and never mentioned the haptic. He listed types of sense impression under the category of 'visual perception' (including illumination, definition, completeness, colouring, extent of field of view). Under 'mental imagery', his examples became more prosaic: are you able to call up an image of printed pages from memory, or 'judge with precision of the effect that would be produced upon the appearance of a room by changing the position of the furniture in it', or 'see the changing positions of troops as *though you saw them on the march* when reading descriptions of battles or manoeuvres', or remember which cards are out of a deck in the middle of a game, or foresee a complicated move in chess?[104] Hearing, smell, and taste are all dealt with summarily, as 'common sense', and there is nothing on touch. For Galton, there was a direct link between these powers of perception and visualisation, and measuring psychological problems. That is, good powers of visualisation equate to good mental function.

For all his faith in the delicate powers of sensitivity possessed by White men, Galton did not trust human capacities: ultimately, no human can be a reliable judge of statistical variation among their own general impressions. In the 1879 paper on 'Generic Images' he argued that however good one's power of visual recall, the mind is a not a technical object, but 'a faulty apparatus for elaborating general impressions' ('Generic Images', p. 533). Statistics can help with these judgements, and in the right proportion, so what was necessary was to deal with

---

[104] Galton, 'Combined Portraits, and the Combination of Sense Impressions More Generally', 26–29 (26).

the facts of general impressions on 'true statistical principles' ('Generic Images', p. 533). Unreasoned impressions are 'necessarily fertile sources of superstition and fallacy from which the child and the savage are never free, and with which all branches of knowledge are largely tainted in their pre-scientific stage' ('Generic Images', p. 534). For Galton, composite portraits are a technique of measurement that can bring about a shift from primitive impressions of children and savages to usable scientific knowledge, a technique as much as a means of understanding the world.

Calculating Degeneracy

Galton's endgame was to apply these tools to generate generic images in eugenic actions: 'Eugenics seeks for quantitative results. It is not contented with such vague words as "much" or "little", but endeavours to determine "how much" or "how little" in precise and trustworthy figures' (*Probability*, p. 13). He moves from general sense impressions that correspond to mental and psychological fitness, to the components that form different types of humans. It is possible to calculate the rate of degeneracy, for example, in children of 'degenerate parents'. If A are those afflicted with degeneracy (determined by personal observation and family history), and B is the offspring of 2 x A, 'of a low average', what Galton wanted to calculate precisely was 'how mischievous will B be to the community?' (*Probability*, p. 13). Let M be the mischief done (mischief is not defined), and D be the 'average amount of the individual deviations from M' (*Probability*, p. 13). D, then, is a measure of untrustworthiness. Based on the calculations of D, measures can be taken against the propagation of class B; that is, against A reproducing.

Underlying these calculations is Galton's worry about keeping up with natural selection, the chaos agent driven by chance, and his primary antagonist. Galton was a Neo-Darwinian in the sense that selection for him, as for Darwin, worked through the individual, not the group. Natural selection does not care about the exception to the rule. This is the reason for urgent intervention, and that there may be other determining factors in evolutionary success does not signify. He is aware of the ethical dangers of the minority report, he says, but this is not as compelling as the evidence that from this combination of 2 x A, selection will produce the mischievous class B, who is unlikely to become a valuable public servant. This is part of Galton's wider case for using composite statistical portraits to make technical judgements about the value of particular human types to a given community. What we can see is the formalisation of certain kinds of difference – behavioural difference in this case – through their measurement.

Galton used the numerical and visual interchangeably; photographs were their own units of measurement in the categorisation of types of humans. Photographs could take the place of numerical points on a statistical graph, and vice-versa: combining portraits of different people into a single image, it was possible to extract the 'typical characteristics' of particular ideal types. Precisely because of his suspicion of individual cognitive faculties, 'the [technological] visualising faculty' was important for this. For him, the composite portrait is a technical, unbiased way of determining averages in balanced ways, so that a hypothesis of type might be proved or disproved, 'pictorial equivalents of those elaborate statistical tables out of which averages are deduced' ('Generic Images, p. 538).

For Galton, using composite portraits to determine average facial expression would offer physiological evidence for the existence of different biological types of humans. In the case of the hereditary basis of criminality, the most important aspect of his investigation into criminal types was to figure out shared expressions and features. Proving the real existence of different human types matters because that is how eugenics can build a society of valuable public servants. The point is to move from the composite through the average to the generic: that is, to prove the existence of a core ideal type. Statistics works by hypothesising about this type, determining averages, and working out whether the data prove the existence of discrete types. He was aware of the danger of producing monstrous, hybrid composite:

> Statistical averages and the like are nonsensical productions unless they apply to objects that cluster towards a common centre; and composite pictures are equally monstrous or meaningless unless they are compounded of objects that have a common similarity to a central ideal type. ('Generic Images', p. 535)

Determining an average is not just an exercise in itself. The average mediates general impression and ideal type. Key here is the idea of a 'common centre' and what this signified. This idea of a common centre has been transplanted into contemporary studies on genomic disease.

Genomic Composites

Genomics is a statistical science. Galton's work on composite portraits was in many ways a historical precedent for some contemporary problems of average and type in genomics, and how the statistical average does or does not correspond to a universal or ideal reference. Since the end of the Human Genome Project, scientists have questioned the usefulness of a composite reference genome. To make the draft reference genome, volunteers were recruited to donate genetic samples. Identifying labels were taken off the samples and destroyed. No record of the labels exists anymore, and there is no way of reconstructing the links between the donors and their samples.[105] The laboratory selected samples at random to make up the reference genome, on the basis that the sequences needed to overlap with each other four-fold. The final average was 4.5-fold, meaning that geneticists had curated an average out of the samples from now-anonymous donors, and this average has since become the standard reference for the human genome against which other genomes are assessed.

Is the human genome a statistical average of a few people, or the ideal reference for *Homo sapiens*? This question has arisen periodically since the early 2000s, and it is particularly charged when it comes to questions of ethnic diversity. In 2012, Jeffrey Rosenfeld, Christopher Mason, and Todd Smith noted that while bioinformatics programmes rely on the current reference sequence, it 'neither adequately represents the full range of human diversity, nor is complete', and that this sometimes leads to invalid assumptions and misidentifications of genetic effects.[106] More recently, after the updated version of the reference genome was released (GRCh38), Xiaofei Yang, Wan-Ping Lee, Kai Ye and Charles Lee pointed out the gaps in the reference genome: 819 to be precise, including minor alleles and errors, and questioned whether it presents common variants from multiple human populations.[107] While some projects have sought to fill in the gaps, most famously the Human Genome Diversity Project, the human reference genome and its updates continue to be the industry standard.[108]

There are not just similarities in how human data are aggregated into an average. Composite images are also used to determine types of disease. Instead of a deviant person, there are deviant genomes. In genomics, the 'type' is not the person, but the disease. One example of this is DNA microarrays, which were developed in the 1990s to look at variations in gene expression. They are glass slides spotted with thousands of biochemical probes on a 2D grid, and they are used most commonly to detect the positions of tumour cells. Like Galton's portraits, microarrays depend on using the composite portrait to make its deviations visible – that is, to calculate the D value, and through this the difference between the average and the pathological. As for Galton, these

---

[105] International Human Genome Sequencing Consortium, 'Initial Sequencing and Analysis of the Human Genome', 860–921.
[106] Rosenfeld, Mason and Smith, 'Limitations of the Human Reference Genome for Personalised Genomics'.
[107] Yang, Lee, Ye and Lee, 'One Reference Genome Is Not Enough'.
[108] See Cavalli-Sforza, 'The Human Genome Diversity Project: Past, Present, and Future', 333–40.

technologies rely on a scientist's power of visualisation, and distinguishing the deviation from standard type. The criminal face is replaced by the diseased genome.

One reason it still matters is that genomics still uses ethnicity data in personalised medicine. These data are often gathered through self-reporting questionnaires that reproduce the same racialised typologies that Galton sorted into a hierarchy of man in *Hereditary Genius*. Why does it matter that these techniques live on in the determination of disease types? Postgenomics is its own composite term, referring at once to the period of time that has followed the first draft sequence of the human genome; the transformation of global bioeconomies that accompanied the novel technologies of the Human Genome Project; and the idea that genomics, which has been accused of reducing body to code, is not enough to understand the complex relation between genetic heredity and genetic expression. In this third sense, postgenomic theories mean not just looking at what we inherit, but also at how our environments shape which parts of the genome might be activated or silenced.

A whole host of identifications and socio-economic interests can be projected onto the gap between statistical average and ideal type. Technologies of sequencing require various shorthands, and often ethnicity, or disability, or sex stand in for precision. Recent historical studies on the methods of genomics and the political economies on which these methods depend have asked big questions about who and what is being privileged in current genomic research, and who will benefit from the results of its findings. Barbara Prainsack and Jenny Reardon approach this question slightly differently and think about the postgenomic as a problem of data interpretation.[109] Genomic diseases are diagnosed by looking at deviations from the reference genome, and genomic methods of disease detection and prediction move between the minutiae of the molecular to the general categories of human still in use in the life sciences, still considered relevant for determining different types of health outcome. This section has explored how these composite technologies of aggregation, visualisation, and detection are embedded in a longer history of visualising inferior or deviant types of humans.

Discussion

Maya: There's a clear connection between this piece and mine. I'm arguing that our archives and our museum collections do not accurately map our history. They seldom include historical traumas and when they do, it is often in

---

[109] See Prainsack, *Personalised Medicine: Empowered Patients in the 21st Century*, and Reardon, *The Postgenomic Condition: Ethics, Knowledge and Justice after the Genome*.

limited or simplistic narratives filtered through a Eurocentric lens. How does this link with the history of postgenomic technologies you are working through?

Lara: It's important to historicise postgenomics' history of visualising hereditary deviance, because this history is a colonial one. Galton spent time in southern Africa, and this was how he came to some of his conclusions about relative intelligence between what he saw as different types of human. One of the problems with centring experience in the biological is that it creates new kinds of essentialisms and exclusions. How do these ways of tracking deviant heredity matter, and to whom? Some of the more interesting science fiction of the twentieth century has taken this conflation of genetics, identity, and capability as its central concern. The digital world that is increasingly ubiquitous in biotech privileges the visual over any other form of perception. This is not the mode in which many other realms of human enquiry function: elsewhere, touch, sound, taste, and smell are just as important as visual perception. Nonetheless, Galton's fixation on what can be perceived and recalled visually continues to shape biotech.

Jerome: If DNA is the 'book' of life, transcribed and transliterated, how might more dynamic and non-linear metaphors of the postgenomic era work themselves through in terms of thinking about history? I'm thinking about Alex and Njabu's idea of 'provenance' and their thinking about challenging 'genealogical' ways of understanding the relationship between now and then.

Lara: Genetics can slice into history at unexpected angles and produce new versions of historical events with forms of data that were inaccessible even twenty years ago. This is a huge shift in the way history can happen. When it's being used like this, genetics is a kind of forensic archaeology. That's where some exciting work on epigenetics is happening, playing a role in excavating histories of colonialism and genocide, and their long-term effects. How might epigenetics offer a counterpoint to the huge sense of loss felt by descendants of these histories? What really happened, whom certain events affected, how many people were involved, who is to blame, which forms of reparation are appropriate or even possible to implement in their wake.

That said, the historical archive matters just as much as any biotechnical rewritings of the past that epigenetics may offer: they should and can be encouraged to work together. I'm based at University College London, which has had its own reckoning with the history of eugenics over the last five years through the Inquiry into the History of Eugenics (2018–2020). One of the big questions in the aftermath has been what to do with the Galton Collection at UCL, which is difficult material to encounter at close proximity, but which offers so many insights into the long-term effects of institutionally validated scientific methods. There is some incredibly rich work coming out of it opening up new directions for historical work on colonialism and racism. The historian Subhadra Das made a podcast series, 'What Does Eugenics Mean To US', which goes into UCL's role in Eugenics in dialogue with academics and public scientists to talk about its influence on – among other things – the concept of death and research in psychology and education, as well as the anti-eugenic work of disability studies. The project, 'Charting a history of eugenics, pre-/ and post-/Galton', led by design researcher Soul Miles and Kaissu Karhu, describes Eugenics as above all a failed utopian design project, which is a good way of putting it. Even if Galton and Pearson failed, the methods created for this project of utopian design still shape present-day imaginaries of future human flourishing, in what can seem like unmarked or apparently a-political forms of aesthetic judgement.

Jerome: You question the precision of statistical accounts of human difference. What does this mean in terms of disciplinary approach, historiography, analysis, and even teaching? What are the lessons we might learn for our understanding of normative knowledge and epistemology here?

Lara: Part of the point of putting history and genetics together is to stress the fallibility of their practices and methods: literally, that they are capable of error, and sometimes these errors are in sync, and sometimes they are in tension. Neither is a static field, and the dynamism of their investigations also shapes the conversation between us in this Element. But when the humanities start talking along these lines, people from other disciplines ask us if all we do is peddle in uncertainty. When the humanities start talking along these lines, sometimes it is difficult to see what purpose these forms of open-ended enquiry serve. Is the function of literature and philosophy to keep a space open for what we can't know about the world? Well, yes; but science also leaves this space open. What we get stuck on, I think, is the usefulness of metaphor and contingency, along with the vertigo of digging up the past: what are we going to find? What are we going to miss? What could a likeness, instead of an exactitude, obscure? Rather than worry about what a poetic approach to science might obscure, I think about this slightly differently: when does a metaphor become an isomorph? That is, when does a figure of substitution become a direct, formal correspondence? This is where the cross-section of metaphor and materiality is important.

Biomedicine is under huge pressure to fine-tune its workings, to offer precision care, to cure the biggest epidemiological problems, and to solve global challenges. When humanities people go into those spaces, it's easy to get swept into this future-orientation, and into the sense that the only kind of time it is really possible to think about is the immediate and up-to-the-minute. But should knowledge production only be directed towards a projected future good, and who will benefit from this? This is an important question that Steve Rose and Hilary Rose ask in *Genes, Cells, and Brains* (2012): *cui bono* – who benefits? Do we know what is going to be good for *Homo sapiens* in 100 years, or 200, or 1,000? Can we trust that the technologies to which human healthcare is becoming increasingly attached will leave a space open for life's vast capacity for error, for trying things out, for embedding past failures into its futures responses, for working out what is relevant in a particular situation? These are questions about how life is valued, and how it is defined. There are valuable lessons to be learned by placing pressure across disciplines, institutions, and public groups to keep asking them.

4 Towards the Rehumanisation of Ancestors from Colonial Contexts at Manchester Museum

Alexandra Alberda and Njabulo Chipangura

Keywords: Mediation/Curation, Provenance, Artefact/Object/Living cultures

Overview

Museums and museum-related institutions are currently grappling with how scientific and colonial epistemologies created injustices in the framework of their own institutions. One area this is evident in is the unethical collecting of 'human remains' that were deposited in museums. Advances in DNA testing and genetics research have been anecdotally suggested to us by non-descendants as methods to connect to living communities. While the intention of these collection practices is often to support the return of remains to their places of origin, this is also an extractive practice, because it takes place without the consent of Ancestors, and is not initiated or led by descendants. In this section, we argue that museums should approach collaboration with Indigenous and descendant communities to rehumanise Ancestors in collections and conduct biographical research as part of repatriation initiative.

Introduction

Manchester Museum (MM) is a university museum in the United Kingdom with a long history as part of the University of Manchester and with colonial collections. The museum has been trying to work in a more socially just way over the last few decades. This approach includes a major repatriation of Ancestors (formerly and widely called 'human remains') which started in the 1990s and moving Ancestors to consecrated stores as part of the process.[110] Our predecessors and later our existing colleagues have been taking the repatriation work forward to include Ancestor and Ancestor-associated material in the early 2000s, secret, sacred, and ceremonial items in 2019 and 2020, all cultural heritage material and specimens in 2023, and current work related to natural history specimens. Throughout this process, the museum and its returning partners have engaged with Indigenous peoples in various ways to consider the return of Ancestors and cultural heritage material. In 2003, then MM Director Tristram Besterman wrote a reflection called 'Returning the Ancestors' that brought together the attitudes, reactions, and experiences at this time.[111] In his reflection we come to see the slowness of museums as relating more to the questions of *power*, *control*, and *use*, more-so-than the technology or methodology to enable return, though ethics stretches across all.

We joined Manchester Museum at a similar time: Alberda was appointed Curator of Indigenous Perspectives in 2021, a new role created by the museum, and Chipangura was appointed Curator of Living Cultures in 2022.[112] We were tasked with culminating the rethinking of collections that the museum has been working towards, Alberda through the Indigenising Manchester Museum (IMM) programme, and Chipangura in reimagining the Living Cultures Collections. Our work includes applying the extent of the United Nations Declaration on the Rights of Indigenous Peoples (UNDRIP, 2007) to centre Indigenous sovereignty, agency, and cultural practices in the work we do. This includes considering how Ancestors are cared for and the rewriting of our Human Remains Policy. Specifically, UNDRIP Article 31.1 pertains to the rights of Indigenous peoples in relation to humanness and genetics:

> Indigenous peoples have the right to maintain, control, protect and develop their cultural heritage, traditional knowledge and traditional cultural expressions, as well as the manifestations of their sciences, technologies and cultures, including human and genetic resources, seeds, medicines, knowledge of the properties of fauna and flora, oral traditions, literatures, designs, sports and traditional games and visual and performing arts. They also have the right to maintain, control, protect and develop their intellectual property over such cultural heritage, traditional knowledge, and traditional cultural expressions.[113]

---

[110] Alberti, *Nature and Culture: Objects, Disciplines, and the Manchester Museum*, p. 109.
[111] Besterman, 'Returning the Ancestors'.
[112] Osman, 'Should Museums Repatriate Stolen Artefacts?'
[113] United Nations Declaration on the Rights of Indigenous People, 2007.

At Manchester Museum we are currently reviewing the place of DNA and the concepts of genetics across our work, including in policies, repatriation, displays, external research requests, proactive provenance of the Ancestors across collections, and learning programmes. In principle, this has developed over the length of MM's history, to our and our colleagues' thoughts today in line with Article 31.1 is that we do not have the rights and rites to determine access, as we are not descendant communities.

In this section we discuss how our work to decolonise and Indigenise our practice has significantly disrupted disciplinarian foundations towards working more collaboratively with communities and collections. We argue that museums cannot avoid critically thinking about how to disengage and reflect beyond Western epistemologies and binaries. We do this by illustrating curatorial practices at MM that are undergirded by community collaborations, inclusivity, critical dialogue and rehumanisation, with examples drawn from our past repatriation work and ongoing provenance and object biographical research.

Colonial Violence and the Dehumanisation of Ancestors

The expansion of the British Empire to Africa, Oceania, Americas, and Asia during colonisation paved way for the violent capture of cultural objects and Ancestors of the colonised that were deposited in museums.[114] As a function of anthropological research, artefacts and Ancestors were separated from their context when they entered museums and were subsequently classified, othered, and categorised according to different disciplines and modes of governance.[115] We reject the view that the primary *use/power* of 'human remains' contained in museums are as devices for 'decoding' history. The dead are Ancestors of living people, and their moral *place* is with their descendant communities.[116] It is also morally wrong to keep Ancestors in boxes and we are of the opinion that their spirits will forever linger restlessly in museum storages until they are properly reburied.

Yann and Mboro (2020) argue that 'in the nineteenth century European anthropologists and colonial officers engaged in a macabre trade of human remains in the name of anthropological science'.[117] These 'remains' still lie restless in museum collections today and are being denied a peaceful afterlife (Gall and Mboro, 'Remembering the Dismembered, 1–3). During colonisation, colonial officers, collectors, and tourists often excavated or took Ancestors from their burial places or as 'trophies' of conflict. The act of collecting them by

---

[114] Chipangura, 'The Benin Tusk and Zulu Beadwork', 106–116.
[115] Bennett, *The Birth of the Museum*. [116] Colwell, *Plundered Skulls and Stolen Spirits*, p. 9.
[117] Le Gall and Sururu Mboro, 'Remembering the Dismembered'.

museums included their display as 'human remains,' and research on them from which information of colonised subjects could be explored through colonial lenses at times to assert White supremacy and evolution.[118] We argue that museums must accept their unquestionable role as conduits of colonial violence with inherited power to organise the world and to shape reality. Some museums continue to display loots of war as trophies of conquest while silencing testimonies of colonial violence. This can be seen in exhibition labels that do not name acquisition history or in 'Our History' webpages that do not tell the truth about connections to transatlantic slavery or other forms of colonial violence when Indigenous and local communities and activists have been protesting for decades for truth-telling and returns. Leaving these objects, histories, or Ancestors uncontextualised when communities call for it is a form of hermeneutical epistemic violence that excludes whole communities and peoples from having the 'knowledge', usually (colonial) academic disciplinary expertise, to participate in culture.[119] For example, in a decades-delayed response to African and Black activists calling for the return of material looted during the British punitive expedition in 1897 from the Kingdom of Benin, including a letter in our own archive from the 1990s from MP Bernie Grant's calls for reparations from British museums, it is only in the last decade that dedicated action has started from British museums.[120]

Colonial violence is entrenched in the structure of what we describe here as the 'encyclopaedic museum'.[121] Colonial violence as part of the punitive and carceral orientations is akin to what Wolfe has called the 'logic of elimination' – part of the settler colonial project which deliberately took aim at appropriating Ancestral remains of the defeated as trophies of conquest.[122] The body of a warrior, especially their missing and stolen parts, was seen as a key historical trope of conquest, with heads separated from bodies and transported across land and sea to European museums.[123] 'Encyclopaedic' museums took shape as global repositories of extracted objects, sites of ordering them according to colonial knowledge, and spaces where the public could acquire knowledge of (and control over) colonised peoples and cultures (Alberti, *Nature and Culture*, 1–14). In this way the establishment of Manchester Museum came from an

---

[118] Biers and Clary, 'Introduction', pp. 1–8.   [119] Fricker, *Epistemic Injustice*.
[120] Pugh, '"We Shall Be Telling our own Stories": Bernie Grant, the Africa Reparations Movement, and the Restitution of the Benin Bronzes', 143–66.
[121] We use the term 'encyclopaedic' to describe how museums in the West benefitted from colonial collections of 'objects and ancestors' that were categorised and classified to prove a supposedly understanding and knowledge of the 'other' in the world through exhibiting their cultures.
[122] Wolfe, 'Settler Colonialism and the Elimination of the Native', 387–409.
[123] Rousseau, Moosage and Rassool, 'Missing and Missed: Rehumanisation, the Nation and Missing-ness, 10–32.

emerging interest in understanding ancient and contemporary worlds from the beginning of the nineteenth century fuelled by Victorian and Edwardian science.[124] Museum collections cannot be separated from power relations inherent in the development of the empire and global colonisation.[125]

Manchester Museum is also complicit in acquisitioning Ancestors during the same period and perpetuating the thinking that supported colonisation.[126] Colonial knowledge produced colonial practices of ordering Ancestors as 'objects' which drew upon Linnaean classification, and informed scientific racism, educational curricula, and legal and administrative frameworks.[127] In pursuit of colonial ordering, material culture was extracted from colonised societies, deprived of its original and contextual meaning, and scrutinised through the lens of colonial knowledge.[128]

The ways in which 'human remains' were deposited into museums as anthropological, archaeological, or even zoological objects points to an active practice of studying the 'other' which substantially dehumanised the identity of the colonised or excavated. Their ontological status as human remains for racial study enabled their transmutation from subject to object and from human to non-human.

Throughout the twentieth century, scientists and museum researchers shifted to extracting different types of information from DNA and bringing genetic research to museum collections. While Colwell was in the University of Manchester it was argued that 'whereas skulls in the colonial context were measured for crude arguments of race – the contemporary study of human remains [could] provide vital insights into environmental change, gender roles, human health, migration patterns, ancestral identities and much more'.[129] Colwell reflects on the establishment of the Native American Graves Protection and Repatriation Act (NAGPRA) in 1990 and how he experienced its conflicted reception:

> Museum professionals feared that the new law would empty their shelves. Native Americans worried that museum people wouldn't really give anything back. A good number of Native Americans had taken to calling trained archaeologists 'looters,' 'thieves,' 'gravediggers.' Many archaeologists grumbled about those Indians stirring up trouble for no good reason at all. It was an education in the ethics of science and the politics of history.

---

[124] Loguno and Merriman (eds.), *The Manchester Museum*.
[125] Soares and Witcomb, 'Towards Decolonisation', 1–8.
[126] Minott, 'The Past Is Now: Confronting Museums' Complicity in Imperial Celebration', 559–57.
[127] Rassool and Gibbon, 'Restitution versus Repatriation: Terminology and Concepts Matter', 1–4.
[128] Muller and Langhill, 'Introduction: How Lively Objects Disrupt Disciplinary Display', pp. 1–23.
[129] Colwell, *Plundered Skulls and Stolen Spirits*, p. 9.

It was also an enigma that was hard to decipher. Why were Native Americans, who want to preserve their culture, so willing to bury it? And how could scientists who spend their lives studying dead Native Americans care so little about living ones? (Colwell, *Plundered Skulls*, 7)

These are still relevant differences of opinions, emotional responses, and feelings today in relation to Ancestors in collections, and specifically the speed at which laws like NAGPRA are implemented. Laws, like NAGPRA,[130] and guidance, such as UNDRIP,[131] set ethical demands and guidance for how Ancestors should be treated and more importantly who are the decision makers over the future of Ancestors. In these and other documents, we recognise the place of descendants, despite what new information could be extracted from Ancestors if they were to remain in collections and used in research. We therefore look at rehumanisation as a function of care not only for the people of history but of a care that extends to communities. This includes promoting Indigenous sovereignty and agency in determining best care for their Ancestors and who they have become to their people. In doing this we concur with Achille Mbembe when he argues that the decolonisation of museums be viewed as an action that seeks to rehumanise by turning human beings that were dehumanised into being humans once again.[132]

Rehumanisation of Ancestors and Curatorial Humility

Across the world, the public-facing work that museums do and their responsibilities towards their collections and constituencies have come increasingly under the spotlight. So, what does the rehumanisation of Ancestors mean to us at Manchester Museum in practice and approach? From an ontological viewpoint, we consider humans as not just living *Homo sapiens*. Humanity extends beyond our lifetime to our remains and in some worldviews beyond our biological material, imbuing Ancestor-associated items, such as cultural material containing human hair or material within which cultural practices imbued a person's spirit. To place this into our practices, we are guided through considering how the privileging of curators as experts and academic knowledge has led to continued forms of colonial violences and injustices in museums. For example, we as curators are often asked to confirm if material is sacred, imbued with spiritual knowledge, or considered an Ancestor or for permission to study an Ancestor and often, researchers have not reached out to Indigenous communities at all. *Curatorial humility* is an epistemological and methodological

---

[130] Native American Graves Protection and Repatriation Act, 1990.
[131] United Nations Declaration on the Rights of Indigenous People, 2007.
[132] Mbembe, 'Decolonizing knowledge and the question of the archive'.

approach that incorporates reconciliation, critical reflexivity and reciprocity with visitors and communities. This allows us to address issues that arise from non-descendants speaking as experts in place of descendants and Traditional Owners, including curatorial silencing, epistemic injustices, and paternalism.[133] In the following we demonstrate how these principles lead our work in rehumanisation.

We argue that repatriations and returning Ancestors are an important form of rehumanisation in the face of multiple layers of dehumanisation. In order to rehumanise, museum staff need to understand the practices and processes that sought to erase the human in a museum (Rousseau, Moosage and Rassool, 'Missing and Missed', 24). As posited by Rousseau et al., this foundation of dehumanisation has rested on tropes of animality by associating certain Ancestors with beings most closely related to humans – monkey, baboon, gorilla. The process of dehumanisation in museums rendered Ancestors as objects of race that were collected, defleshed, classified, studied, and exhibited. Stripping all human dignity even in death by subjecting Ancestors to different kinds of practices, such as measuring, othering, and racial profiling is part of the dehumanisation process.

In order to move beyond epistemic cultures of ordering and objectifying Ancestors, Manchester Museum is seeking to learn from previously marginalised Indigenous knowledge to challenge colonially derived curatorial practices. Various approaches have been suggested for museums as they engage with local communities from where objects were dislocated and categorised in accordance with colonial epistemes.[134] These include co-creation, co-production, social inclusion, and co-curatorship in museum spaces. Drawing from work from across the museum over the last decade, our approaches have been centred around the application of relational curatorship as both a method and concept that we are using in reconciling continued colonial violence in the collections.

In that respect Manchester Museum is progressively transforming into a space that promotes inclusion to facilitate conversations about *meanings* of collections rather than presenting them as *materialities* of Western-ordered cultural knowledge. This includes moving beyond seeing provenance research as a legal obligation in repatriation processes, which can be used to support or deny requests from descendant communities, or desk-based research pulling from existing colonial or institutional narratives. Leading from a curatorial humility approach, we acknowledge the historical racism, paternalistic privileging of academia that enabled testimonial and hermeneutical injustices that

---

[133] Alberda 'Graphic Medicine Exhibited', p. 178.
[134] Oswald, *Working through Collections*, p. 5.

actively excluded Indigenous peoples and non-academics from sharing their experiences and knowledge.

Manchester Museum's new approach to curatorship is a profoundly relational practice of caring for collections through active relations and dialogue with our diaspora and descendant communities. Brown states that museums and activism can come together to provide communities sites to work collectively, build sustainable relationships, and promote well-being.[135] We hope to learn from activist-led responses to collections through these socially engaged practices. Through emphasising the ethics of care, inclusion, and imagination Manchester Museum has begun to rethink the collections collaboratively increasing in the last decade. A commitment to inclusion means greater collaboration and co-production and foregrounding diverse perspectives so that we become relevant to these communities. Imagination underscores an engagement with big ideas, bringing people together to tell stories and to explore important questions and research.[136] Our value of care is at the heart of acknowledging the role that colonial violence played in ordering our collections as we look at what it means to care for people, their ideas, and their relationships with these 'objects' and 'specimens' which acknowledges they are a part of living cultures and kinships. All these values directly speak to our pragmatic approach in doing decolonial work as we advance the notion that whilst museums are about collections – museums are also about people.[137]

Museum objects become more extraordinary when they connect with people in active curatorial relationships and practices of meaning making. This we refer to as relational curatorship which we have embraced Manchester Museum as a decolonial practice. With imagination, the Ancestors and objects we care for help to build understanding between cultures and a more sustainable world (Ali, 'Esme Ward', 2). In relational curatorship Ancestors and objects are not treated as frozen nor ordered in a timeless past but are reordered as living beings connected to the present and future in continuous ongoing relationships.[138] They connect people, places, and events. Equally, they represent histories of continuity and change. By using relational curatorship as both a theory and method, we seek to reimagine a curatorial practice that is more inclusive and open to views from communities that were subjected to different forms of colonial violence and regimes of global ordering, including testimonial and hermeneutical injustices. In our attempt to re-order knowledge using relational curatorship, we recognise and address communities as experts, sources of

---

[135] Brown, 'Museums and Local Development', 1–13.   [136] *Manchester Museum Guidebook*.
[137] Ali, 'Esme Ward (Manchester Museum): In Conversation', 1–3.
[138] Golding and Modest, 'Thinking and Working through Differences: Remaking the Ethnographic Museum in the Global Contemporary', p. 93.

knowledge and different ways of knowing, and provenance research partners who hold agency and cultural authorities about their heritage and Ancestors. As such, we pay them for their contributions, aim to foster long-term relationships, and create projects from their current needs.

Relational practices that we describe address the silencing that colonial and Western perspectives that predominately frame interpretations of Ancestors and objects in museums. In catalogues, objects, including objectified Ancestors, are presented using Western-centric interpretations that do not recognise the ways in which they are enmeshed with spiritual and religious cultural practices or their everyday significance from the perspectives of communities of origin. The social life incorporating functions, meanings, and status that they have passed through in the course of their usage is often ignored.[139] However, one cannot decolonise a museum without delinking its colonial matrix of power since the practice of collecting, classifying, and cataloguing objects is deeply embedded in colonialism itself which created the museum institution as we know it today.[140] Looking at Ancestors, we argue here that spiritually, death does not sever the link between the living and the dead, and that death does not strip us and our descendants from the rites of consent or cultural sovereignty. Rehumanisation directs that Ancestors who are contained in encyclopaedic museums should be given the posthumous respect they deserve. This approach also points to a practice of making the museum a place that can give new life to the conquered or those whose descendants are still in the act of resistance. By extension reburials and returns symbolically confers posthumous citizenship to the missing Ancestors.

We suggest a practice of curatorial humility which acknowledges that museums are becoming more critical of their colonial past by diffusing curatorial authority into a shared practice that recentres Indigenous and diaspora community aspirations. We interrogate the notion of care to signify the relationships between objects and people as facilitated by curators in challenging exclusions of people whose cultures are represented and othered in museums.[141] With Ancestors, we cannot gain their consent or perspectives. This matters to us because we recognise their humanity. We work towards reconciliation with descendant communities, though at times we face challenges and confront ourselves in starting and maintaining these relationships, to build practices that reciprocate their needs.

---

[139] Appadurai, 'Introduction', pp. 1–12.
[140] Mignolo, 'Museums in the Colonial Horizon of Modernity', pp. 71–85.
[141] Marstine and Hing Kay, 'Curating Art as a Relational Practice', pp. 1–18.

Rethinking Manchester Museum's Ancestral/Human Remains Policy

In view of ongoing discussions around the rehumanisation of Ancestors in our collections Manchester Museum is currently reviewing its Ancestral/Human Remains Policy. The redefined policy seeks to acknowledge that Ancestors we care for were unethically 'collected' from Africa, Asia, Oceania, and the Americas through grave robbery, punitive expeditions, pseudo-anthropological/science research, looting, and military conquests. In doing so we seek to initiate proactive steps in engaging communities in the restitution of unethically acquired Ancestors and their respectful treatment by everyone concerned. We view the rewriting of our current humans remains policy as a major strand of our decolonial work with the hope of facilitating purposeful and proactive acts of return (Rassool and Gibbon, 'Restitution versus repatriation', 2). Significantly, we wish to highlight in this policy that if we conclude from own our research that a repatriation is due, and that we will not wait for a claim to be made but rather proactively seek to initiate a dialogue with potential descendants. We will acknowledge that all repatriations, despite the willingness of museums and the care of their staff to do right, are conversations of loss, ownership (in a legal sense) and histories. While we are still considering how these acknowledgements will translate in this intended practice, our ambition is that we are trauma-engaged, one of our IMM principles, so that we recognise trauma but move beyond to promote healing and Indigenous agency instead of another wave of injustice and saviourism.

In rewriting the current Policy we are led by the following new principles both developed from the changing values at Manchester Museum (care, imagination, inclusion) and in response to changing social discourses and Indigenous calls to actions to museums. This will also have to be in view of the UK government guidance for the *Care of Human Remains in Museums*[142] as this will have an influence on how we frame the new policy. While it is still in development, and an important upcoming phase of work will include external stakeholders, we hope the following ethical positions are reflected in the new policy:

A. Recognise and respect 'human remains' as Ancestors of living people.
B. Acknowledge that 'human remains' were once part of living people and that many people feel a personal connection with particular Ancestors, whether through genealogical descent, location or personal belief.

---

[142] Care of Human Remains in Museums, UK Government, assets.publishing.service.gov.uk/media/5f291770e90e0732e4bd8b76/GuidanceHumanRemains11Oct.pdf.

C. Care for the Ancestors in our collection in a respectful manner that is culturally specific.
D. Consult with appropriate groups of people when making decisions about particular Ancestors.
E. Accept that the collection of 'human remains' was a process that dehumanised people and seek to rehumanise unethically collected remains in our collections.

To this end, our commitment to rehumanisation is premised on a deep understanding that 'human remains' are considered unethical if:

1. They were collected and used for the purpose of racial study.
2. They were removed from graves of individuals who were known-in-life or are named individuals recorded in the accession book/register.
3. They were collected through grave robbery, body theft, or illicit activity.
4. They were collected via trade or exchange locally or internationally and collected as trophies.

The call for rehumanisation for us working with problematic 'objects' and Ancestors stems from a profound desire to acknowledge coherent persons subjected to disruptions in life, who were further inserted into racial history in death, and to return not just the remains but the person, the human (Rousseau, Moosage and Rassool, 'Missing and Missed', 29).

Unconditional Repatriations as a Decolonial Methodology

We regard unconditional repatriations as a decolonial methodology that is informed by approaches based on open disclosure combined with proactive strategies of identifying Ancestors who were subject to one or more of the previously mentioned unethical conditions that we hope will be defined in the new policy. By taking this truth-telling initiative, museums do not have to wait for claims to come from communities who might not be aware of what we hold in our collections (Chipangura, 'The Benin Tusk and Zulu Beadwork', 113). In view of the unconditional repatriation approach, we posit that although decolonial work has been critiqued extensively as essentially epistemological and somewhat slowly becoming a metaphor – the work that Manchester Museum has been doing now significantly points towards the direction of empirical decolonial engagements.[143] For the last decade, Manchester Museum leadership has believed that every repatriation is not an end but a chance for a new beginning. In order for that to happen our IMM work continues to think how

---

[143] Kassim, 'The Museum Will Not Be Decolonised', 1–14.

trauma-engaged principles enable us to do this work sensitively. Soares and Witcomb succinctly argue that 'by acknowledging coloniality in museums, we must therefore assume that decolonisation is an ongoing process that involves restitution and rehumanisation, notably through the sharing of knowledge and by encouraging mutual understanding' (Soares and Witcomb, 'Towards Decolonisation', 2).

The repatriation process is much more than just a legal or material transfer of objects, natural specimens or Ancestors back to communities – rather, it is a restoration and return of spiritual and sacred knowledge that may have been previously lost as a result of colonial violence and associated appropriating methods. It is also important to underscore that in some instances communities do not demand to have everything back from European museums but desire to be connected with their collection with the aim of recovering lost Indigenous knowledge and working towards cultural revitalisation (Soares and Witcomb, 45'Towards Decolonisation,' 1–8). Although decolonisation in Europe is now synonymously associated with calls for the repatriation of cultural objects and Ancestors, it is crucial to understand that what precedes any form of return is an understanding of the history of the collection and its association with colonialism with the aim of improving our knowledge on its provenance (Savoy 2022). We agree that the returning of Ancestors is an important decolonial call in museums, and we believe that the process of returning is much more than a physical movement to the original place of life. Rather, the process we are developing is centred on the restoration of personhood that turns Ancestors into humans again as part of the return.

Conclusion

For communities it is essential to understand that reclaiming back their lost heritage through repatriations signifies a reconnection with their history. We have suggested that rehumanisation of Ancestors in museums can restore their dignity by challenging how they were treated as objects in collections. We have also articulated our positions on Indigenous peoples and descendant communities maintaining agency over their own Ancestors, in terms of both the knowledge they contain and their physical care. In this respect, we suggest that colonial museums, situated outside of Indigenous communities, do not have the authority to determine the use of DNA testing and rather should approach provenance from the point of view of social biographies, curatorial humility, and relational curatorship. For us genetics thus centres on re-ascribing Indigenous agency, as outlined by UNDRIP, and rehumanising Ancestors through a decolonial approach to provenance research to recontextualise the posthumous lives of these individuals and work towards reconciliation. We are not naive in thinking that creating positive relationships, some decolonial practices, and repatriations *alone* will truly reconcile the violence towards peoples, Ancestors and descendants that having them in our collections does. However, we hope that we can work in ways that promote healing by not centring on the museum in decision-making and acknowledging in our actions how racialised history and science drove the dehumanisation of Ancestors for the benefit of Western worldviews and research. Shifting agency to Indigenous peoples to determine how and where their Ancestors should be cared for, and how we get there with a more humanised approach, is our intention at Manchester Museum.

Discussion

Maya: I find that much of what gets written about changing practices doesn't refer to or describe the way that for decades Black and Global Majority people have been lobbying museums to behave in more ethical ways or take restorative action on past colonial harm. The result implies that museums themselves have decided to move to more respectful and ethical ways of working when in fact they often actively resisted or ignored requests and demands from community members.

Alex: Agreed. I find working in this sector today, there is a lot of emphasis on the history of museum development, but sometimes this loses sight of the social context outside of it. A part of that is addressing our own past and the active decisions people made previously to ignore or resist community members.

Njabu: Alex has precisely touched on very important issues that we are grappling with as museum professionals from the Global Majority as we question problematic histories associated with collections from colonial contexts. What is lacking is an understanding that these 'objects' of the 'other' have underlying social biographies that are connected to living local communities. Confronting these exclusions curatorially comes from our willingness to share authority. Today a curator is a facilitator of dialogue wherein Black and Global Majority people are given agency to explore meanings of their own living cultures that have been imprisoned in museum dioramas for a long time.

Jerome: Can you elaborate about the idea of provenance as an historical research approach?

Njabu: Provenance research takes much more than tracing the legal history of an object but rather is a quest to understand underlying collecting histories and colonial contexts of acquisitions. At Manchester Museum we have been approaching this question methodologically by opening our unprovenanced African collections to the diasporans of African heritage and working with them through shared knowledge production. I also want to underscore here that provenance research work cannot be separated from the biographical search which we are also conducting collaboratively with descendant and diaspora communities in Manchester.

Lara: Does 'rethinking' the museum mean having to have proof or documentary evidence that certain things happened? What kinds of pressure does this place on descendants and non-descendant activists to do sometimes impossible work (because this evidence might not exist, or the only evidence is that a particular object/artefact is within the collection)?

Alex: Personally, I believe it is the responsibility of museums to make time and provide resources for this work when needed. We don't want to repeat colonial violence by returning an Ancestor to the wrong communities because we didn't do our due diligence in the provenance process nor rely on processes of (re)traumatisation of descendants to do this work. We are working to be more proactive and seeing how far we can take provenance research without having to put that burden on descendants. We are also working at a governance level to embed more ethical practice and ideas of 'evidence' in view of understanding that the presence of the Ancestor shows grave robbing or violence happened.

Jerome: I'm really interested in the idea of rehumanisation and how it intersects with other (genetic) work on the idea of the 'human'. Can you say something more about the idea of the 'human' as a material and genetic being in history?

Njabu: The act of rehumanisation in museums addresses how both Ancestors and living cultures from the colonised were dehumanised by racial studies. What then does it take to be human again where we treat Ancestors with respect, dignity and at the same time restore the biographical life of objects? The answer is: in a decolonial moment Ancestors are not material manifestation of a particular historical time that are waiting to be measured, sampled, studied and genetically analysed. Instead they are living and for example in an African worldview spirits of the dead will forever linger restlessly in museum storages until the Ancestors are properly reburied.

Jerome: Could you expand a bit on the ethical dimensions of your approach?

Alex: Trauma-informed practices acknowledge and seek to understand colonial violence and their continued impact when working with communities; trauma-engaged practices take it a step further to consciously try to create healing and needs to be relational. Ethical practices and positions are a way to assert our actions against epistemic injustices and are ways to confront the parts of ourselves as individuals or our disciplines we haven't yet critically engaged with.

Njabu: For me the ethical dimension of practicing decolonial work is informed by a self-reflection of my own curatorial approach through honesty, transparency, openness, and truth-telling. That's the entry level to practicing an ethic of care as curator of living cultures working in solidarity with communities in co-producing new narratives and meanings with them and not for them.

Lara: Your section brings up so many questions around data collection methods and their associated technologies. Can 'secularised' methods of collecting and identifying biodata facilitate the forms of psychic, spiritual, and sacred reparations that return involves?

Alex: I think the answer to that question will be deeply personal and come from individual's own relationship to the histories of science and continued feelings of extractive research practices and museums. It needs to be up to communities to determine if collecting and identifying biodata is a method they are comfortable with, which for some may provide the reparations you describe. We would not lead on or offer, due to our work understanding what colonial violence our museum was a part of with 'sampling' and racialised science, but we would respect the ambitions of descendant communities.

Endings

Here we reflect upon the process of developing this work and outline how we have responded to the central set of concerns that emerged from our collaboration. Partly this was driven by the development of our central Keywords: **Mediation/Curation, Provenance, Measurement, Influence, Metaphor, Artefact/Object/Living Cultures**. Foregrounding these concepts allowed us to conceptualise the overlap between our approaches and our understanding.

Jerome

For me, the true collaboration between academic and practitioner approach has been the most valuable and the most difficult aspect of this work. This collaboration allows us to think about authority and to challenge how it has worked in the past. Our multiplicity of approach has enabled us to think outside of standard structures.

This is crucial. Without this collaboration the humanities are increasingly isolated. We need to think about what in an email to me Lara called 'knowledge production in and by communities and diverse publics'.

DNA is a multiple concept that touches various different aspects of historical practice, from preservation to articulation. As a metaphor and as a materiality it provides us in this Element with a prompt to think carefully about various ways we approach and understand the past.

I wonder, too, about the ideas of 'failure' in that we raise in the introduction. I'm not sure that it is the right term. We have produced something complex and multilayered, seeking to bring as much in as possible and to avoid imposing normative ideas of stability and order.

I think that crucially, we need to open up clearer lines of communication between those working in archives, museums, and libraries, and those working in university disciplines. As this Element shows, the cutting-edge work being done in museums and heritage sites reflects the needs and challenges of communities, rethinking anti-racist practices through collaboration. This is something that is still very much lacking in many university departments, and we need to learn from our colleagues about the different types of ways that we should be engaging with and learning from the communities we work within. In particular, I think we need to learn much more about co-production, about challenging extractivist discourses (particularly those implemented by the university itself), about listening, and about humility. The contemporary neoliberal university is too swift to see 'outreach' as something of a quick fix rather than a long-term restitutive, reparative set of actions. Bringing the practices and approaches, and ethos, of our colleagues in museums and heritage spaces to bear on work in the university would lead to meaningful entanglement, actual impact, and the reconfiguring of knowledge so as to be liberating and equitable rather than negative and copyrighted.

Maya

This collaborative endeavour has been challenging in some respects. Collaboration takes more time than solo work, and we are all busy people. Our approach has required a flexibility and an openness in our writing and a willingness to let go of control – by this I mean letting go of the desire to wrestle with the sections to extract obvious points of contact between each and every piece. For all the challenges, I think we have created something interesting, creative, and worthwhile. There are some very clear connections between the pieces; we have also allowed ourselves the freedom to spin off in other directions too.

I entered the project hyper-conscious of my non-academic standing. I don't work within the academy; I haven't studied academically beyond undergraduate level. I could, however, draw on my significant experience working in and with

Global Majority communities and heritage organisations, as well as our recent research If Nothing Change, Nothing Changes. I was upfront with my colleagues about my intent to write in a simple and direct way that feels comfortable to me, even if that might feel uncomfortable for academic readers.

My piece approaches DNA in a fairly straightforward way, using it as a metaphor. Through this I offer a historiographical reading of the UK heritage sector's collecting and working with collections, and how this maintains a Eurocentric and colonial way of looking at the world. By offering examples of the Ahmed Iqbal Ullah Education Trust's approach to contemporary archival collecting and of centring Global Majority histories I offer new ways of working that will create collections in more equitable and anti-racist ways. Collections created in this way will in turn allow more equitable and anti-racist ways of telling our collective stories, which can only improve the way we approach our histories.

My section points towards a new approach to collecting and collections, which decentres traditional gatherers and holders of knowledge, by bringing in and centring voices and perspectives that have been marginalised, omitted, or silenced. In a similar way, our unusual collaboration mirrors this, and points to a new way of presenting ideas and knowledge. I believe we have shown how our different ways of writing and exploring ideas about history and pinning down understandings of who we are results in a nuanced, complex, and rich work which readers will find stimulating.

Lara

How far is genomics from the history of eugenics, and what does this imply for practicing scientists, genetic counsellors, and historians of science? My section considered a history of measurement that continues to be important in current genomics via Galton's invention of 'pictorial statistics'. Statistical modelling is commonly used in genomics to determine the loci of genetic abnormalities and disorders. To detect an abnormality, you need a 'normal' reference point for comparison. Tracing a link between Galton's attempts to correlate features into a statistical composite of particular human 'type' and the human reference genome means that I can explore how the idea of biological type was embedded in a racial logic. For Galton and Pearson, the 'race' category was loose: it encompassed what now corresponds to ethnicity, but it also included poets, whom Galton did not think made reliable public servants. Galton wanted his legacy to be a contribution to improving Britain for the better, promoting the reproduction of valuable public servants.

Genomics is very far from the kind of language that Galton used, more likely to talk about types of disease than types of humans. Nonetheless, ethnicity data continue to be used to determine the prevalence of certain disorders or abnormalities in certain communities, or whole continents. Race thinking is alive and well in the pre-emption, diagnosis, and treatment of particular health issues in Europe and North America, and in global practices in genomic research. Twentieth-century medicine learned many lessons about the arbitrariness and danger of applying categories of ethnicity too loosely, or too broadly, without taking many other possible factors into account: environment, lifestyle, or shock events to which an organism has to respond. Heredity is just one of these factors.

Alex and Njabu

Not actively disrupting colonial histories, legacies, and Western-centrism in policies is one way epistemic violence continues in museums. Restitution and repatriation are how we can answer calls to be accountable from Indigenous, diaspora and originating communities and activists, as Maya highlights in her section. In reviewing our Ancestors/Human Remains Policy at Manchester Museum, our ambition is to embed relational, decolonial, and de-westernised practices that mean we are more prepared for meaningful reconciliation and steps towards healing. As a university museum in the UK, our own history is deeply embedded in the use of collections to further research and 'knowledge'. Provenance research, as a historical practice, is one avenue for showing how continued-coloniality impedes social justice through collections today. Our previous version of this policy had started to address stakeholders that need to be consulted that extended beyond academics to communities; however, it was not an equitable approach to whose voices, direction, or needs were at the centre. This no longer is the case across our different practices as we show accountability to the colonial mindsets and practices that dictated that an Ancestor's, labelled as human remains, value was in there academic and scientific study. Any policies we have will still have to adhere to the UK law and university processes. However, we are confident that through these and changing attitudes and research priorities beyond our cultural sector that our ambitions are possible. As highlighted across the different authors' contributions and discussions, there are varied approaches to considering how DNA, genetics, and history are changing and being taken in new directions that do not rely on the continued violence against Ancestors or their descendants' healing processes.

Bibliography

Abel, Sarah, *Permanent Markers* (Chapel Hill: University of North Carolina Press, 2021).
Ahmed, Sara, *Complaint!* (Durham, NC: Duke University Press, 2021).
Alberda, Alexandra P., 'Graphic Medicine Exhibited', Doctoral Thesis Submitted to Bournemouth University, 2021, 178.
Alberti, Samuel, *Nature and Culture: Objects, Disciplines, and the Manchester Museum* (Manchester: Manchester University Press, 2009).
Ali, Roaa, 'Esme Ward (Manchester Museum): In Conversation', *Cultural Trends* 32:4 (2023), 1–3.
Alpaslan-Roodenberg, Songül, Anthony, David, Babiker, Hiba, et al., 'Ethics of DNA Research on Human Remains', *Nature* 599 (2021), 41–46.
Anderson, Warwick, 'Decolonizing Histories in Theory and Practice', *History & Theory* 59:3 (2020), 369–75.
Appadurai, Arjun, 'Introduction', in *The Social Life of Things*, ed. Arjun Appadurai (Cambridge: Cambridge University Press, 1986), 1–12.
Ballouz, Sara, Dobin, Alexander and Gillis, Jesse A. 'Is It Time to Change the Reference Genome?' *Genome Biology* 20:159 (2019), https://doi.org/10.1186/s13059-019-1774-4.
Basch, Corey H., Joseph Fera and Nasia Quinones, 'A Content Analysis of Direct-to-Consumer DNA Testing on TikTok', *Journal of Community Genetics* 12 (2021), 489–92.
Basu, Paul, 'Material Culture: Ancestries and Trajectories in Material Culture Studies', in *The Handbook of Socio-Cultural Anthropology*, ed. James G. Carrier and Deborah B. Gewirtz (London: Routledge, 2020), pp. 370–90.
Basu, Paul, 'Towards the Pluriversal Museum: From Epistemic Violence to Ecologies of Knowledge', *Museums and Social Issues* 18 (2024), 1–16, https://doi.org/10.1080/15596893.2024.2333658.
Behm, Amanda, Christienna Fryar, Emma Hunter et al., 'History on the Line: Decolonizing History', *History Workshop Journal* 89 (2020), 169–91.
Benn Torres, Jada, 'Genetic Anthropology and Archaeology', *PaleoAmerica* 2:1 (2016), 1–5.
Benn Torres, Jada, and Gabriel A. Torres Colón, *Genetic Ancestry* (London: Routledge, 2021).
Bennett, Tony, *The Birth of the Museum* (New York: Routledge, 1995).
Besterman, Tristram, 2003. 'Returning the Ancestors', tinyurl.com/5587mw3h.

Bibliography

Biers, Trish and Katie Stringer Clary, 'Introduction', in *The Routledge Handbook of Museums, Heritage and Death*, ed. Trish Biers and Katie Stringer Clary (London: Routledge, 2024), 1–8.

Bolnick, Deborah A., Jennifer A. Raff, Lauren C. Springs, Austin W. Reynolds and Aida T. Miró-Herrans, 'Native American Genomics and Population Histories', *Annual Review of Anthropology* 45 (2016), 319–40.

Booth, Thomas, 'A Stranger in a Strange Land', *World Archaeology* 51:4 (2019), 586–601 (590).

Brace, Selina, DIekmann, Yoak, Booth, Thomas J., et al., 'Ancient Genomes Indicate Population Replacement in Early Neolithic Britain', *Nature Ecology & Evolution* 3 (2019), 765–71.

Brown, Karen, 'Museums and Local Development', *Museum International* 71:3–4 (2019), 1–13.

Cavalli-Sforza, L. Luca, 'The Human Genome Diversity Project: Past, Present, and Future', *Nature Reviews Genetics* 6 (2025), 333–40.

Chilunga, Felix, Henneman, Peter, Venema, Andrea, et al., 'DNA Methylation', *Epigenomics* 13:9 (2021), 653–66.

Chipangura, Njabulo, 'The Benin Tusk and Zulu Beadwork', *Museum Anthropology* 46:2 (2023), 106–16.

Chipangura, Njabulo, and Jesmael Mataga, *Museums as Agents for Social Change* (London: Routledge, 2021).

Chipangura, Njabulo, and Motsane Seabela, 'Community Collaborations and Social Biographies of Museum Collections from Colonial Contexts: Meanings of Zulu Beadwork', *Museum Worlds* 12 (2025), 16–30.

Chipangura, Njabulo, and Patricia Chipangura, 'Community Museums and Rethinking the Colonial Frame of National Museums in Zimbabwe', *Museum Management and Curatorship* 35:1 (2022), 36–51.

Colwell, Chip, *Plundered Skulls and Stolen Spirits* (Chicago, IL: University of Chicago Press, 2017).

Dawkins, Richard, *The Selfish Gene* (Oxford: Oxford University Press, 2006 [1976]).

de Groot, Jerome, 'The Genealogy Boom', in *The Impact of History? Histories at the Beginning of the 21st Century*, ed. Bertrand Taithe and Pedro Ramos Pinto (London: Routledge, 2015), 21–34.

de Groot, Jerome, *Double Helix History* (London: Routledge, 2023).

Egorova, Yulia, 'DNA, Reconciliation and Social Empowerment', *British Journal of Sociology* 69:3 (2018), 546–51.

Elkins, Caroline, *Legacy of Violence* (London: Vintage, 2023).

Etges, Andreas, and David Dean, 'The International Council of Museums and the Controversy about a New Museum Definition – A Conversation', *International Public History* 5:1 (2022), 1–4.

Faulks, Sebastian, *Seventh Son* (London: Penguin, 2023), 231.

Fowler, Corinne, *The Countryside* (Harmondsworth: Penguin, 2023).

Fox, Keolu, 'The Illusion of Inclusion', *The New England Journal of Medicine* 383 (2020), 411–13.

Fox Keller, Evelyn, *A Feeling for the Organism* (London: St. Martin's Press, 2000 [1983]).

Fox Keller, Evelyn, 'From Gene Action to Reactive Genomes', *Journal of Physiology* 592:11 (2014), 2423–29.

Fricker, Miranda, *Epistemic Injustice* (Oxford: Oxford University Press, 2007).

Frieman, Catherine, Anne Teather and Chelsea Morgan, 'Bodies in Motion: Narratives and Counter Narratives of Gendered Mobility in European Later Prehistory', *Norwegian Archaeological Review* 52:2 (2019), 148–69.

Furholt, Martin, 'Massive Migrations?' *European Journal of Archaeology* xxi (2018), 159–91.

Galton, Francis, *Hereditary Genius* (London: Macmillan, 1869).

Galton, Francis, 'Combined Portraits, and the Combination of Sense Impressions More Generally', *Proceedings of the Philosophical Society of Birmingham* 2 (1879), 26–29.

Galton, Francis, 'Generic Images', *Popular Science Monthly* 15 August 1879, 532–44.

Galton, Francis, *Inquiries into Human Faculty and its Development* (London: J.M. Dent, 1883).

Galton, Francis, 'Eugenics, Its Definition, Scope and Aims', *The American Journal of Sociology* 10:1 (1904), 1–25.

Galton, Francis, *Probability, the Foundation of Eugenics* (Oxford: Clarendon Press, 1907).

Gates, Henry Louis, Jr., *In Search of Our Roots* (New York: Random House, 2009), 10.

Geography Now, 'My DNA Heritage Test Results (I Was Shocked)', 8 May 2022, youtube.com/watch?v=G_IdpTRlTt8&ab_channel=GeographyNow.

Gissis, Snait, 'Interactions between Social and Biological Thinking', *Perspectives on Science* 17:3 (2009): 237–306.

Golding, Viv, and Wayne Modest, 'Thinking and Working through Differences: Remaking the Ethnographic Museum in the Global Contemporary', in *Curatopia: Museums and the Future of Curatorship*, ed. Phillip Schorch and Conal McCarthy (Manchester: Manchester University Press, 2019), pp. 90–106.

Green, Monica, 'Taking "Pandemic" Seriously', *The Medieval Globe* 1 (2014), 27–61.

Haak, Wolfgang, Lazaridis, Iosif, Patterson, Nick, et al., 'Massive Migration from the Steppe', *Nature* 522 (2015), 207–11.

Hakenbeck, Susanne E., 'Genetics, Archaeology and the Far Right', *World Archaeology* 51:4 (2019), 517–27.

Hammonds, Evelynn, 'Straw Men and Their Followers', in *Beyond Bioethics*, ed. Osagie K. Obasogie and Marcy Darnovsky (Oakland: University of California Press, 2018), pp. 403–409.

Hanson, Clare, *Genetics and the Literary Imagination* (Oxford: Oxford University Press, 2020).

Hedenstierna-Jonson, Charlotte, Kjellström, Anna, Zachrisson, Torun, et al., 'A Female Viking Warrior Confirmed by Genomics', *American Journal of Biological Anthropology* 164:4 (2017), 853–60.

International Human Genome Sequencing Consortium, 'Initial Sequencing and Analysis of the Human Genome', *Nature* 409 (2001), 860–921.

Johanssen, Niels N., Greger Larson, David J. Metzler and Marc Vander Linden, 'A Composite Window into Human History', *Science* ccclvi 356 (6343) (2017), 1118–20.

Karp, Ivan, and Corrie Kratz, 'The Interrogative Museum', in *Translating Knowledge: Global Perspectives on Museum Community*, ed. Raymond Silverman (New York: Routledge, 2014), 279–99.

Kassim, Sumaya, 'The Museum Will Not Be Decolonised', *Media Diversified* 11/15 (2017), 1–14.

Keats, John, 'Hyperion', in *The Major Works*, ed. Elizabeth Cook (Oxford: Oxford University Press, 2008), ll. 173–74.

Kenney, Martha, and Ruth Müller, 'Of Rats and Women', *BioSocieties* 12 (2017), 23–46.

King, Laura, and Gary Rivett, 'Engaging People in Making History', *History Workshop Journal* 80:1 (2015), 218–33.

Kirshenblatt-Gimblett, Barbara, *Destination Culture, Tourism, Museums and Heritage* (Berkeley: University of California Press, 1998).

Kleinburg, Ethan, Joan Wallach Scott and Gary Wilder, 'Theses on Theory and History', *History of the Present* 10:1 (2020), 157–65.

Kristiansen, Kristian, Allentoft, Morten E., Frei, Karin M., et al., 'Re-theorising Mobility and the Formation of Culture', *Antiquity* xci (2017), 334–47.

Landecker, Hannah and Aaron Panofsky, 'From Social Structure to Gene Regulation, and Back', *Annual Review of Sociology* 39:1 (2013), 333–57.

Larsen, Clark Spencer, *Bioarchaeology* (Cambridge: Cambridge University Press, 2015 [1997]).

Laughlin, Robert, *A Different Universe* (London: Basic Books, 2007).
Le Gall, Yann, and Mnyaka Sururu Mboro, 'Remembering the Dismembered', Doctoral Thesis Submitted to the University of Potsdam, 2020.
Leroux, Darryl, *Distorted Descent* (Winnipeg: University of Manitoba Press, 2019).
Lester, Alan, *Deny and Disavow* (London: Sun Rise Books, 2022).
Lewis-Kraus, Gideon, 'Is Ancient DNA Research Revealing New Truths?' *New York Times Magazine* 17 January 2019, nytimes.com/2019/01/17/magazine/ancient-dna-paleogenomics.html.
Lichtenstein, Alex C., 'Decolonizing the AHR', *American Historical Review* 123:1 (2018), xiv–xvii.
Lloyd, Sarah, and Gary Rivett, 'Fraught Spaces', *Rethinking History* 27(4) (2023), 602–636, https://doi.org/10.1080/13642529.2023.2255770.
Loguno, Dimitri, and Nick Merriman, eds., *The Manchester Museum* (Manchester: The Manchester Museum, 2012).
M'charek, Amade, *The Human Genome Diversity Project* (Cambridge: Cambridge University Press, 2005).
Manchester Museum Guidebook (London: Scala and Heritage, 2023).
Marcon, Alessandro R., Christen Rachul and Timothy Caulfield, 'The Consumer Representation of DNA Ancestry Testing on YouTube', *New Genetics and Society* 40:2 (2021), 133–54 (133).
Marrati, Paula, and Todd Myers, 'Introduction', in *Knowledge of Life (Forms of Living)*, ed. Georges Canguilhem, trans. Stephanos Geroulanos (New York City: Fordham University Press, 2008), xvii–xx.
Marstine, Janet, and Oscar Ho Hing Kay, 'Curating Art as a Relational Practice', in *Curating Art*, ed. Janet Marstine and Oscar Ho Hing Kay (London: Routledge, 2022), 1–18.
Mbembe, Achille, 'Decolonizing Knowledge and the Question of the Archive,' Lecture delivered at the Wits Institute for Social and Economic Research, 2015, http://tinyurl.com/4aedcych.
Merrill Squier, Susan, *Epigenetic Landscapes* (Durham, NC: Duke University Press, 2017).
Mignolo, Walter, 'Museums in the Colonial Horizon of Modernity: Fred Wilson's Mining the Museum (1992)', in *Globalization and Contemporary Art*, ed. Jonathan Harris (New Jersey, NJ: Wiley-Blackwell, 2011), 71–85.
Minott, Rachael, 'The Past Is Now: Confronting Museums' Complicity in Imperial Celebration', *Third Text* 33:4–5 (2019), 559–57.
Muller, Lizzie and Caroline Langhill, 'Introduction: How Lively Objects Disrupt Disciplinary Display', in *Curating Lively Objects*, ed. Lizzie Muller and Caroline Langhill (London: Routledge, 2022), 1–23.

Nelson, Alondra, 'The Social Life of DNA', *British Journal of Sociology* 69:3 (2018), 522–37.

Osman, Erin, 'Should Museums Repatriate Stolen Artefacts?' *The Mancunion*, 23 November 2023, tinyurl.com/mr3cdsn3.

Oswald, Margareta, *Working through Collections: An Ethnography of the Ethnographic Museum in Berlin* (Leuven: Leuven University Press, 2022).

Panofsky, Aaron, and Joan Donova, 'Genetic Ancestry Testing among White Nationalists', *Social Studies of Science* 49:5 (2019), 653–81.

Prainsack, Barbara, *Personalised Medicine: Empowered Patients in the 21st Century* (New York: New York University Press, 2017).

Pravinchandra, Shital, 'One Species, Same Difference?' *New Literary History* 47:1 (2016), 27–48 (28).

Price, Neil, Hedenstierna-Jonson, Charlotte, Zachrisson, Torun, et al., 'Viking warrior women?' *Antiquity* 93:367 (2019), 181–98.

Pugh, Cresa L. '"We Shall Be Telling our own Stories": Bernie Grant, the Africa Reparations Movement, and the Restitution of the Benin Bronzes,' *Politique Africaine* 1 (2022), 143–66, https://doi.org/10.3917/polaf.165.0143.

Rassool, Ciraj, and Victoria E. Gibbon, 'Restitution versus Repatriation: Terminology and Concepts Matter', *American Journal of Biological Anthropology* 184(1) (2023), 1–4.

Reardon, Jenny, *Race to the Finish* (Princeton, NJ: Princeton University Press, 2005).

Reardon, Jenny, *The Postgenomic Condition: Ethics, Knowledge and Justice after the Genome* (Chicago, IL: University of Chicago Press, 2017).

Reardon, Jenny and TallBear, Kim, '"Your DNA Is Our History": Genomics, Anthropology, and the Construction of Whiteness', *Current Anthropology* 53:S5 (2012), S233–S245.

Reich, David, *A Brief History of Everyone Who Ever Lived* (London: Weidenfeld & Nicolson, 2017).

Rheinberger, Hans-Jörg, and Staffan Müller-Wille, *The Gene* (Chicago, IL: University of Chicago Press, 2017).

Richardson, Sarah, *The Maternal Imprint* (Chicago, IL: University of Chicago Press, 2021).

Richardson, Sarah, and Hallam Stevens, *Postgenomics* (Durham, NC: Duke University Press, 2015).

Rosenfeld, Jeffrey, Christopher Mason and Todd Smith, 'Limitations of the Human Reference Genome for Personalised Genomics', *PLoS ONE* 7:7 (2012), https://doi.org/10.1371/journal.pone.0040294.

Rousseau, Nicky, Riedwaan Moosage and Ciraj Rassool, 'Missing and Missed: Rehumanisation, the Nation and Missing-ness, *KRONOS* 44 (2018), 10–32.

Rutherford, Adam, 'Introduction', in *How to Argue with a Racist*, paragraph 6, Kindle edition (London: Weidenfeld & Nicolson, 2020).

Sailiata, Kirisitina, 'Decolonization', in *Native Studies Keywords*, ed. Stephanie Nohelani Teves, Andrea Smith and Michelle H. Rahjeta (Tucson: University of Arizona Press, 2015), 301–308.

Saini, Angela, 'Stereotype Threat', *The Lancet* 395:10237 (2020), 1604–605 (1604).

Sandahl, Jette, 'Curating across the Colonial Divides', in *Curatopia, Museums and the Future of Curatorship*, ed. Phillip Schorch and Conal McCarthy (Manchester: Manchester University Press, 2019), 72–89.

Sanghera, Sathnam, *Empireland* (London: Viking, 2021).

Smith, Laurajane, *Uses of Heritage* (London: Routledge, 2006).

Smith, Laurajane, 'Heritage, the Power of the Past, and the Politics of Misrecognition', *Journal for Theory of Social Behaviour* 52 (2022), 623–42.

Soares, Bruno, *The Anti Colonial Museum: Reclaiming our Colonial Heritage*. London: Routledge, 2023).

Soares, Bruno, and Andrea Witcomb, 'Towards Decolonisation', *Museum International* 74:295–96 (2023), 1–8.

Sommer, Marianne, *History within* (Chicago, IL: University of Chicago Press, 2016).

TallBear, Kim, *Native American DNA* (Minneapolis: University of Minnesota Press, 2013).

Tsosie, Krystal S., Keolu Fox and Joseph Yracheta, 'Genomics Data', *Nature* 591:529 (2021), https://doi.org/10.1038/d41586-021-00758-w.

Tuck, Eve, and K. Wayne Yang, 'Decolonization Is Not a Metaphor', *Decolonization* 1:1 (2012), 1–40.

Vander Linden, Marc, 'Population History in Third-Millennium-BC Europe', *World Archaeology* xlviii (2016), 714–28 (714).

Vawda, Shahid, 'Museums and the Epistemology of Injustice: From Colonialism to Decoloniality', *Museum International* 71:281–82 (2019), 72–79.

Verges, Françoise, *A Programme of Absolute Disorder: Decolonizing the Museum* (London: Pluto Press, 2024).

wa Thiong'o, Ngũgĩ, *Decolonising the Mind* (Oxford: James Currey, 1986).

Wade, Peter, 'Race, Multiculturalism, and Genomics in Latin America', in *Mestizo Genomics: Race Mixture, Nation, and Science in Latin America*, ed. Peter Wade, Carlos López Beltrán, Eduardo Restrepo and Ricardo Ventura Santos (Durham, NC: Duke University Press, 2014), 211–39.

Wailoo, Keith, Nelson, Alondra and Lee, Catherine, 'Introduction' in *Genetics and the Unsettled Past*, ed. Keith Wailoo, Alondra Nelson and Catherine Lee (New Brunswick, NJ: Rutgers University Press, 2012), 1–12 (7).

Wailoo, Keith, Alondra Nelson and Catherine Lee, eds., *Genetics and the Unsettled Past* (New Brunswick, NJ: Rutgers University Press, 2012).

Watson, James, 'Growing up in the Phage Group' (The Biological Laboratories, Harvard, 1966).

Watson, James, *DNA* (London: Orion, 2012 [1968]).

Watt, Elizabeth, and Emma Kowal, 'What's at Stake?' *New Genetics and Society* 38:2 (2019), 142–64.

White, Chris, *Museums and Heritage Tourism: Theory, Practice and People* (London: Routledge, 2024).

Wolfe, Patrick, 'Settler Colonialism and the Elimination of the Native', *Journal of Genocide Research*, 8, 4 (2006), 387–409.

Yang, Xiaofei, Wan-Ping Lee, Kai Ye and Charles Lee, 'One Reference Genome Is Not Enough', *Genome Biology* 20 (2019), https://doi.org/10.1186/s13059-019-1717-0.

Yehuda, Rachel and Amy Lehrner, 'Intergenerational Transmission of Trauma Effects', *World Psychiatry* 17:3 (2018), 243–57.

Younge, Gary, 'Obituary: Ambalavaner Sivanandan', *The Guardian*, 7 February 2018, theguardian.com/world/2018/feb/07/ambalavaner-sivanandan.

Zhang, Sarah, 'Ancient DNA Is Rewriting Human (and Neanderthal) History', *The Atlantic*, 14 March 2018, https://goo.gl/LEVsEv [accessed 27 March 2018].

Zhu, Yujie, *Heritage Tourism: From Problems To Possibilities* (Cambridge: Cambridge University Press, 2021).

Zimmerer, Jürgen, Friederike Odenwald and Kim Sebastian Todzi, 'Displacing the Objects of Others: Towards a Holistic Approach in (Post-) Colonial Provenance Research', in *Displacing and Displaying the Objects of Others: The Materiality of Identity and Depots of Global History*, ed. Jürgen Zimmerer, Kim Sebastian Todzi and Friederike Odenwald (Berlin: de Gruyter, 2024), 3–31.

Acknowledgements

Thanks to Daniel Woolf for commissioning and supporting us throughout.
Thanks to Clare Hanson for being wise and prompting us to rethink our key ideas.
Thanks to Krystal Tsosie for outlining her important work at an early stage of the development of the project.
Thanks to everyone at CUP involved in editorial and production.

Maya: Thank you to my colleagues in the Ahmed Iqbal Ullah Education Trust Coming in from the Cold team: I've learnt so much from their sensitive and community-centred archiving practice. And importantly, to the very many Global Majority activists who persistently demand more and better of the heritage sector.

Alex and Njabu: Thank you to Georgina Young, Head of Collections and Exhibitions at Manchester Museum, for your leadership bringing rehumanisation and Indigenisation to the forefront of rethinking collections, and supportive and critical feedback on our section. And, to Esme Ward, Director, and Stephen Welsh, former Curator of Living Cultures, who both have been instrumental in the inception of Indigenising Manchester Museum and African provenance work. To all communities and staff we work with.

Jerome: Thanks to Bria Cotton, Liv McCafferty, Keisha Thompson, Jo Yee Cheung, Petter Hellström. My work was supported by a Fellowship at the Swedish Collegium for Advanced Study in Uppsala. Thanks to Christina Garsten, Mattias Bolkéus Blom, Bjarne Graff, Pia Hultgren, Maria Odengrund and all the SCAS staff. Thanks also to my fellow Fellows Ester, John, Jonathan, Arthur, Jenny, Desiree, Hannah. Thanks to Mattias Jakobsson, Tobias Gunther, Helena Jankovic Malmström, Tina Saupe and the Evolutionary Biology group.

Lara: Thanks to Liliane Campos, Anne Duprat, Julia Jordan, Florian Mussgnug, Susan Merrill Squier, and Stephen Shapiro.

Cambridge Elements

Historical Theory and Practice

Daniel Woolf
Queen's University, Ontario

Daniel Woolf is Professor of History at Queen's University, where he served for ten years as Principal and Vice-Chancellor, and has held academic appointments at a number of Canadian universities. He is the author or editor of several books and articles on the history of historical thought and writing, and on early modern British intellectual history, including most recently *A Concise History of History* (CUP 2019). He is a Fellow of the Royal Historical Society, the Royal Society of Canada, and the Society of Antiquaries of London. He is married with three adult children.

Editorial Board
Dipesh Chakrabarty, *University of Chicago*
Marnie Hughes-Warrington, *University of South Australia*
Ludmilla Jordanova, *University of Durham*
Angela McCarthy, *University of Otago*
María Inés Mudrovcic, *Universidad Nacional de Comahue*
Herman Paul, *Leiden University*
Stefan Tanaka, *University of California, San Diego*
Richard Ashby Wilson, *University of Connecticut*

About the Series
Cambridge Elements in Historical Theory and Practice is a series intended for a wide range of students, scholars, and others whose interests involve engagement with the past. Topics include the theoretical, ethical, and philosophical issues involved in doing history, the interconnections between history and other disciplines and questions of method, and the application of historical knowledge to contemporary global and social issues such as climate change, reconciliation and justice, heritage, and identity politics.

Cambridge Elements

Historical Theory and Practice

Elements in the Series

Plural Pasts: Historiography between Events and Structures
Arthur Alfaix Assis

The History of Knowledge
Johan Östling and David Larsson Heidenblad

Conceptualizing the History of the Present Time
María Inés Mudrovcic

Writing the History of the African Diaspora
Toyin Falola

Dealing with Dark Pasts: A European History of Auto-Critical Memory in Global Perspective
Itay Lotem

A Human Rights View of the Past
Antoon De Baets

Historians' Autobiographies as Historiographical Inquiry: A Global Perspective
Jaume Aurell

Historiographic Reasoning
Aviezer Tucker

Pragmatism and Historical Representation
Serge Grigoriev

History and Hermeneutics
Paul Fairfield

Testimony and Historical Knowledge
Jonas Ahlskog

Race, Genetics, History: New Practices, New Approaches
Alexandra P. Alberda, Njabulo Chipangura, Lara Choksey, Jerome de Groot and Maya Sharma

A full series listing is available at: www.cambridge.org/EHTP

Printed by Integrated Books International,
United States of America